Selling Information

How YOU can create, market and sell knowledge in ANY field?

FRED GLEECK

– *First Edition* –
Fast Forward Press • Henderson, NV

If you find typographical errors in this book they are here for a purpose.
Some people actually enjoy looking for them and we strive to please
as many people as possible.

Selling Information

How YOU can create, market and sell knowledge in ANY field!

By Fred Gleeck

Published by:

Fast Forward Press
209 Horizon Peak Drive
Henderson, NV 89012
702-617-4205 – phone
fgleeck@aol.com
www.fastforwardpress.com

Cover design and interior layout © Nick Zelinger, NZ Graphics
znick4@qwest.net

ISBN: 0-936965-48-7

contents

My $97 GIFT for YOU!
Just for joining my list!

I want to give you something that really is worth $97. Why would I do this? Because I want you to allow me to keep this conversation we've started going. That's right, it's a BRIBE to let me stay in touch with you.

If you're willing to give me your email address I'll send you a transcript of one of my bootcamps that I normally sell for $97. It's yours with no strings attached. If you ever get tired of my sending you information (which I hope NEVER happens), all you have to do is click the UNSUBSCRIBE button that comes with every email that I send out.

I know you already get tons of emails and you hate most of them. This won't be true with what I send you. You'll get a series of great take away information that you can put to use immediately. Do what it says on each page and send an email to tips@sellingInfoProducts.com

Introduction to Information Products

My name is Fred Gleeck. I have an unusual background.

I was born in Japan and raised in the Philippine Islands. My dad was stationed overseas with the Foreign Service as an American Diplomat, which is why I ended up growing up there. My passion, while I was growing up in the Philippines, was to become a professional golfer. So, I played golf almost every day of my life. I was considered to be a very good player in the Philippines, but when I came back to the United States, I realized that I couldn't shine shoes for most of the people that were here playing college golf. So, I went to college and got a degree in Marketing and Psychology and then got a Masters Degree in International Business. After graduate school I moved to New York City, turned 22 years old, and was promptly fired by 5 major US corporations in a row!! This proved conclusively that I should be self-employed.

In the early 1980's, I took a few seminars from a guy named Howard Shenson who then became my mentor. Howard conducted seminars on a number of topics including: "How to Start Your Own Consulting Business" and "How to Market and Promote Your Own Seminars and Workshops." I do seminars and have written books on the same two topics. Because of these seminars and Howard Shenson's tutelage, I started to do a lot of off-line marketing of my information products.

In 1984, soon after getting fired for the last time, I gave my first "open to the public" seminar at the Saddle Brook (New Jersey) Marriott outside of New York City. I had about 45 people show up for a seminar called "How to Start and Build Your Own Consulting Business." I made about $2200 that day. Not bad money for the mid 80s.

I gave that seminar without ever having done a day's worth of consulting in my life. I'm not suggesting you do the same because it's a little bit disingenuous. I did, however, read 70 books on consulting and therefore felt qualified to deliver the material.

When people would ask me a question at the seminar, I would give some very articulate answer that was based entirely on reading, not experience. Most importantly, I already had something to sell during that first seminar. None of what I offered for sale was mine, but I did have something to sell. That changed very quickly.

Before the end of 1984, I had developed numerous products of my own. I currently make a very large percentage of my total income from the sale of my own information products. One of the things I'm going to teach you in this book is how to create and market different types of products. When we talk about creating, marketing and selling informational products, we're talking about all different kinds of products including books, ebooks, audios, videos, seminars, telesminars, bootcamps, etc.

In 1985 I produced one of the first infomercials in the information marketing field outside of the real estate arena. I lost a ton of money but my then partner went on to sell close to a BILLION dollars worth of products and services via infomercials. I lost thousands of dollars, but he got a hell of an education.

Right now, I have over 150 different web sites and I serve 10 primary niche markets. I have niches from self-storage to catering to video producers to limousine drivers. I have created a different line of products for each of these 10 market niches. (I'll cover niche marketing and the need for it later.) Most of the systems that I am employing now are web-based, and you'll read about the need to do that as well. This book will show you the exact techniques that I use and are working in the niche markets that I have chosen.

Are you ready to learn how I do it? This book starts with a little bit of background, and then goes into the actual "how-to" of product creation. After I show you how to create the information products, I'll show you how to sell them.

Fasten your seat belts!

DEFINITION OF
an INFORMATION PRODUCT

So, what's an information product? It's any product or service that you can sell to people to provide them with information, usually about a specific topic. Sounds redundant, but that's it! Information includes, but is not limited to, books, e-books, CD ROMs, audios, videos, seminars, tele-seminars, coaching, consulting - any kind of information that you can sell in ANY form. It's a catch-all term that covers a large number of possible options. Remember, when we use the term product, we use the term loosely. In this book, it's going to represent either a product or a service.

Why Sell Information Products?

So, why do I sell information products and why should you? It's fun. I love sharing my knowledge with other people. I love to see people start to make a bundle of money from the information that I provide for them. If you've got a topic that excites you and you believe in, then you, too, can get into the game of marketing information products.

Beyond the fun is the money. Let's talk about why it makes "money sense" to get into the business of marketing these kinds of products. First of all, the margins are incredible compared to most other products or services. For example, let's take a cassette tape of a seminar that will retail for $197. The actual cassettes cost no more than fifty cents a piece. Add a little bit more for a workbook and a manual. My total cost in this program might be around eight dollars. Now $8 as a total cost when you're selling something for $197 produces very fat margins. Over 20 to 1. Those are the kinds of margins we have in the information products business.

It doesn't take a lot of sales with those kinds of margins to make money.

In the example above I used audio cassettes to illustrate the point. Whether you sell audio tapes, CD-roms, MP3's or any other audio format, your margins will be similarly large. In most cases, even larger!

I've been involved with other businesses with slim margins and I can tell you that they are not for me. And that's what we're looking to try and do - create huge margins. Information products allow us the luxury to create those kinds of margins. Selling information products is an incredible business to be in. What other business can you produce something for $5 (or even less) and sell it for $100 and have people begging you for more? And that's why the information product line is so attractive, because you don't have to sell a whole lot of products to make a very, very nice profit.

If you've got knowledge about a particular subject, or just the passion to research a topic, chances are you can sell that knowledge and get paid handsomely for it. It virtually doesn't matter what your field of expertise is. Someone out there wants to know more about it!

Selling information products also allows you, when set up properly, to make money while you sleep. In many businesses you get paid for your time. In the information products business, you produce something once and get paid forever. Well, almost! What I mean is that it is not uncommon for me to wake up in the morning and find that I have generated over five, six, or even seven hundred dollars worth of orders in one day. Sometimes I have made as much as $3,200.00 in orders on a given day for various kinds of information products without my having to lift a finger.

Once the system is set up, it can be an ongoing source of income. And that's what I think is so valuable. I know your time will be much better spent pursuing other activities once you've set up a system that is automatically generating money. You can be finding other niches, perhaps creating other products, doing all kinds of other things. So it's a "make money while you sleep" business, as well.

Another benefit is that selling information products makes you an expert and authority in the field of your choice. If you have information products in a given area, you instantly become the "de facto" expert on that topic. This is true especially if you have a book on the topic since books have a higher perception of authority than other products such as audios or videos. However, all of the different kinds of information products help to elevate your status within a marketplace and make you the presumed expert in that field.

Most importantly, however, selling information products can help you live a great life and maintain a great lifestyle. My goal is to maintain my apartment in the New York City area, my house in Las Vegas, and next summer, I want to spend a couple of months in Europe as well. My goal is to spend winter in Las Vegas, drive to New York City to spend the summer and fall and then interrupt my New York City stint with a trip to Europe in July and August.

I want to travel with my dogs and cat. I don't need big residences in each of these places, but I like the idea of being able to spend my time where I want to spend it. Selling information products is allowing me to live my dream life. That's what's important to me. Now, for you, having multiple residences may not be important, and that's fine. Whatever your goals are, you can achieve them through the system you will read about in this book.

Right now, I still have to send out (or have my fulfillment house send out) audio and videotapes and people get a physical product in their hand. In the future info marketers will be selling "hybrid" products. When people order they will immediately receive some digital component of the product. Soon thereafter they will receive the balance of the product package in a physical form. Doing things this way will satisfy a customers need for immediate gratification AND also allow you to put a physical product in their hands. This is what the future of info marketing will bring.

The physical product will always be important. There are two major reasons why it's so crucial to continue to have a physical component to your packages. First, people want to put their hands on something PHYSICAL when they spend their money. Second, it dramatically reduces return rates. It is a much bigger hassle for people to have to pack things up, put them in a box and then send them back to take you up on a guarantee.

No matter how "high tech" the world gets, people will still want and PAY FOR physical products and experiential events. Experiential events include seminars, bootcamps and the like. People will always want and pay to have physical contact with friends and experts in their fields.

As bandwith increases and technology advances, many things will change. Many more information products will be digitally delivered, but many things will remain the same. People will always want to buy products with a physical or experiential component.

Selecting a Market: You Need to Select a Niche

Before you begin selling products, you need to select a niche market. Selecting a niche market is crucial to your success as an information marketer. If you're trying to sell to everyone, you will sell to no one. You need to select some kind of a specific niche.

How do you determine, then, what your niche should be? Well, you should take a look first at your background. What is your personal background? Your academic background? Your social background? Are there areas that make you stand out from the crowd? This will help you to discover what you already have inside of you in terms of your knowledge, your abilities, your interests, and your inclinations – any of these might be possible niches.

Be sure to look at your work background. Too many people discard this area because they disliked their job so much. Consider taking the job that you hated for so long and turning it into an information product! If you've been working in a full time job, don't think that just because you're going to get into the information products business that now you shouldn't use that background.

I have one client who is a chiropractor. He likes the business but doesn't want to be working as many hours as he now does. So, I'm helping him design a series of information products for other chiropractors who are equally frustrated with the amount of hours they have to work. A thriving info-products business will allow him to work less hours but stay in the field he loves.

Take a look at your personal interests. What do you like? Create information products that are based on your interests.

Most importantly, however, you only want to work on products where you have a passion. Why would that be? Because if you don't, what happens? It's boring. It's uninteresting. It's not exciting. It's not fun. We don't want to do any of that if we're getting into an information products business. If you are passionate about a topic, it becomes easier for you to generate the materials, to do the work to get it all done. It's critically important to feel that level of passion.

The niche must also be big enough to warrant your time. Before you really start targeting a niche, let me give you this story. I had a client for a few years who is a periodontist. There are approximately 5,500 periodontists in the United States. This client, much to my regret, has tried to sell information products to that group at the $100 level (which I'll explain in a moment). Even assuming he got every single person in that group to order, he still couldn't make enough money to make it worth his while.

If you did have a niche that had 5,500 people in it, I'm not saying you shouldn't go after it. I am saying, however, that you certainly shouldn't go after it with low-end products. So, if you have 5,500 people in your niche, you might try to attack them with a much higher product (two, three, four, ten thousand dollar), since your market is so limited.

In order to determine if your niche is large enough, you need to look at two things – the total number of buying units and their ability to pay. The total number of buying units is how many people are out there that can buy your products and services. My own rule of thumb is that you shouldn't pursue a niche unless it has at least 40,000 buying units.

Now let's take a look and try to understand the difference between the total number of units and the total number of buying units. In the self-storage industry for example, there are over 33,000 facilities in the United States. That's the total number of facilities. However, there are about 21,000 or 22,000 buying units. Why is there a discrepancy between those two numbers? Some people own more than one!

Let's take another example. I have a client who's trying to market products to the "rent-to-own" niche. Similar to self-storage, one person might own four of those rent-to-own locations; therefore, all four of those would be considered one buying unit.

Chances are that if someone owns three of these storage unit facilities, they are not going to buy three sets of materials. They're going to buy one unit and copy them for their other locations. Even though they're not allowed to do this because of copyright laws, you should assume that is what they're going to do anyway. If they were a very large organization, however, (there is one self-storage facility that owns over 1,200 units) they wouldn't risk making copies because getting caught would open them to the potential of getting slapped with a huge copyright infringement lawsuit. (This is where you would have the opportunity to LICENSE them a set of materials.) So, just understand that, in terms of buying units, the number of buying units is potentially very different from the total number of units.

You've taken a look at the total number of buying units in your niche. Now you also need to look at their ability to pay. Do these folks that you're targeting have a strong ability to pay and a desire to pay and a willingness to pay for whatever products you're going to create? Do they have the means, and do they have the inclination to buy the products and services that you're going to offer them?

Some people will assess this opportunity inaccurately. For example, there is a very well known person in the self-publishing field who once told me "people like authors and publishers won't spend BIG money to attend an event". I've proven him wrong repeatedly. Don't base your decision on what you think; base it on tests and results. Find out whether or not your market can tolerate and support the prices and the services that you're going to sell.

The next thing you need to do is determine whether the niche you are considering has an upward or downward trend line associated with it. It this niche shrinking or expanding? In the next three to five years do you see more or less people coming into this niche? If it's not an expanding niche, be careful!

Additionally, you'll have to ask yourself whether this niche has a decent turnover rate. Are new people coming into the niche. This is different from the direction the niche is headed. How much new blood is coming into the niche. The more, the better. Why? Because then more people can buy what you have to sell!

Can you find the folks that you're going after quickly and easily? Do they have a regular publication? Can you rent their names from a list broker? The easier to find and get to these people, the better the niche would be.

Where are the folks in this niche located geographically? Does it matter to you that many of them are outside the United States? Does is matter to you that half of them are in Alaska? Consider the physical location of the niche. Why? When you start doing consulting work or seminars and training, will you want or find it easy to go to these places?

You need to find the right niche. I'm not saying you can't go after everyone and be successful, but I am saying that's a very difficult thing to do. It takes a lot of marketing dollars, a lot of effort and a lot of PR. I would suggest that you get your start first with a specific market niche.

Now, didn't I just break my own "rule" by pursuing a niche like self-storage that only has 20k+ buying units? Yes. Rules are sometimes made to be broken. Self storage operators happen to be a niche that are VERY willing to spend money on these kinds of products so I bent my own rules and targeted them. Good thing. It's become a VERY profitable niche for me.

You can take a mass-market topic, however, and niche it. For example, let's say you wanted to create a book on sales. Well, "sales" is a pretty mass-market topic. You might consider sales for engineers - you know: how to sell as an engineer. To do this, you take your topic and even without changing the title of it, you niche it sort of naturally. There's one gentleman that I'm coaching right now who's doing a product that's very motivational. His background is in the high tech field so he's specifically targeting the high tech field with his message. He took a mass-market message (motivation) and targeted it to a specific niche: high tech. Even if your goal is to sell to the mass-market, I suggest that you pick a specific niche or two first.

Do not rule out anything you are interested in. I'm never surprised by niche market possibilities! Did you know that there are 250,000 rabbit breeders in the country? There are four trade publications for the rabbit breeding industry. Vintage pens? There's resurgence in interest in vintage pens. Surprising? Hardly.

The sex industry is a perfect example of the ultimate niche marketing. There is a fan club for every fetish out there. A friend of mine is really brilliant. She was able to start a sex toys business. She became an affiliate for a site and because she knew how to drive traffic to the site, she made over $12,000 last month - just off that one site alone! Just from directing people to her affiliate site. I'm not here to discuss the morality of these markets, I'm just here to explain how they work.

I'm a Libertarian; what people do or don't do is their business. That's their privilege, but what a great money making opportunity for my friend!

I'm in the process of launching a site for myself right now that relates to one of passions – film. The site is www.TalkinHollywood.com. The goal is for the site to become THE place where everyone interested in movies goes to find out the latest. I hope to attract "regular" people like you and me, but also, the actors, producers and directors in the Hollywood community.

I know this will be a success because I have a passion for film and I've also got a good model. The original idea came from a new friend of mine who runs www.TalkinBroadway.com. Yes, I basically "stole" the idea from him.

There's nothing wrong with your doing something similar. Just make sure you don't copy their content and ALWAYS remember to give credit where credit is due.

There's a niche for everyone. And do you know what? You just need to figure out what your niche is and go after it. NOW.

information Product Creation

Some Basics

Don't try to make your products perfect. Some of you reading this book are probably perfectionists and you like to make sure that everything is perfect before you do it. Trust me, nothing you ever produce will ever be perfect! That's why at the front of every one of my books I put in a line that says "IF you find typographical errors in this book, they're here for a purpose. Some people actually enjoy looking for them and we strive to please as many people as possible".

You have to realize that whether it's a book or an audio program or videotape, etc., whatever you produce is not going to be perfect. Get over it. If you want it to make something prefect, you're living in the wrong world. Use the "ready, fire, aim" approach to creating products. This is the only way you'll make any money.

I'm not saying that you should produce shoddy products. What I am saying is that content should triumph over the production value of your product. I want you to produce really, really strong content because strong content will overrule any marginal levels of mistakes that you make in other areas of your information products. Your goal with every product you create is to make people feel that they got at least ten times what you charged them for the product or service in value. So, make sure that your content is incredibly strong. People will forgive little mistakes in production values.

If you were to reverse that idea and design a beautiful product that was beautifully packaged but the content was lousy, your customers won't forgive that. That doesn't mean to say that over time your product shouldn't be perfected, but even in the act of perfecting your product, I want you to be careful. Why? Because if something looks too good, it's hard to charge as much money for it.

Let me repeat that. If something looks too good and too slick, it's hard to charge as much money for it. Why? Due to something that I call the "Nightingale-Conant Syndrome. " Nightingale-Conant is one of the largest producers of informational products in the country, in fact, in the world. They have very, very beautifully packaged, four-color audiocassette binders that sell for about $60 for six cassette tapes. We are not trying to look like them because our price points are going to be so much higher. (I'll explain price points just below). We sell our audio cassettes for up to $197 per set and MORE. We don't want to try and compete at $60 per set – our profit margins are much better than that.

But we want our product(s) to look a little bit like it came out of a back room somewhere – like it was created by some kind of a mad scientist. That's the kind of look we're going for here. We're not going for an ultra-fancy look. If you give something to someone that looks too fancy they will start to associate it with those others firms that are producing inexpensive products with fancy four color covers. So you want to look good but you don't want to look too good. Additionally, slick looking products tend to intimidate your audience.

You also need to keep in mind that people learn through different modalities. This is incredibly important for you to understand. Although you may like to attend seminars, your clients and customers may prefer to learn in a different way. Some people like to read, other people like to watch, some people like to listen, still other people like to experience. The people who like to experience may like to experience in person or over the phone.

So when you're creating your line of information products, you want to do so in such a way to accommodate each one of those individuals. This means you'll need to produce books, e-books and reports for those who like to read. For those who prefer to learn by listening, you'll want to create audiotapes, CD ROMs and downloadable audio files. For those who like to watch, you'll need to produce videos and DVD's and online video. And finally, for those who like to experience, you'll want to provide seminars, bootcamps, and tele-seminars.

Funnel System

If all this makes sense to you so far, you are ready to understand something that I call the FUNNEL SYSTEM. The funnel system is my model for selling your information products. First, you need to create a skeletal line (initially) of information products. Second, you have to fill the funnel with quality leads at the least possible cost. Then you have to get those people to buy something from you - usually a relatively low cost product. Finally, you have to sequentially (and automatically) trade customers up to higher and higher priced products and services.

When people don't know who you are, your chances of selling them a high-priced product is relatively slim. The more often you have contact with people and the more personal that contact, the better your chances are of selling them more expensive items. After they buy the first product, your goal is to trade them up to more and more expensive products and services. In a nutshell, you need to produce products using different modalities of learning at different price points ranging from a low of $10 to a high of $1,000.

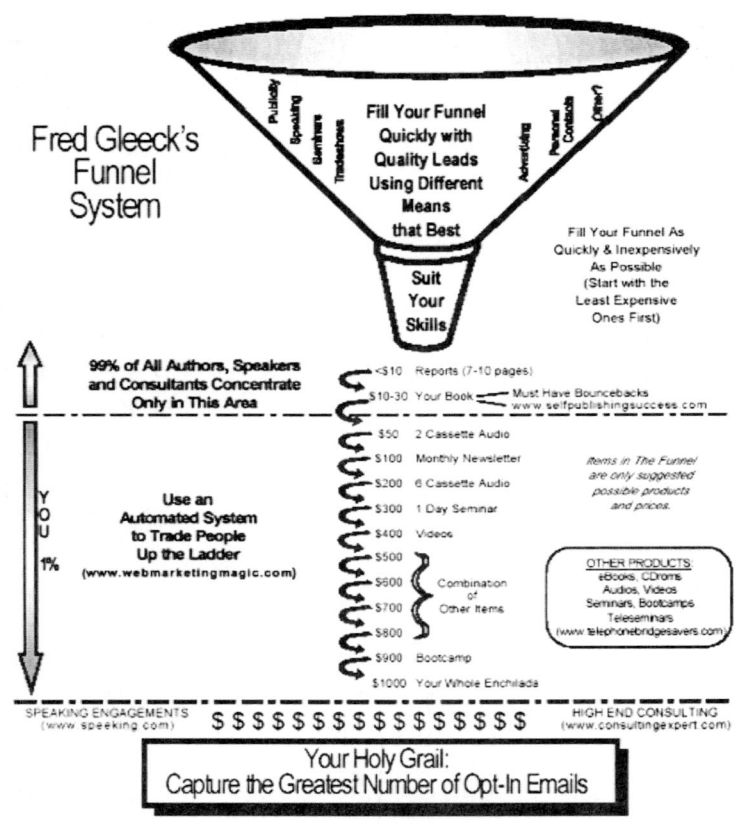

Fred Gleeck's Funnel System

Fill Your Funnel Quickly with Quality Leads Using Different Means that Best

Suit Your Skills

Fill Your Funnel As Quickly & Inexpensively As Possible (Start with the Least Expensive Ones First)

99% of All Authors, Speakers and Consultants Concentrate Only in This Area

Use an Automated System to Trade People Up the Ladder (www.webmarketingmagic.com)

<$10	Reports (7-10 pages)	
$10-30	Your Book	Must Have Bouncebacks www.selfpublishingsuccess.com
$50	2 Cassette Audio	
$100	Monthly Newsletter	Items in The Funnel are only suggested possible products and prices.
$200	6 Cassette Audio	
$300	1 Day Seminar	
$400	Videos	
$500		
$600	Combination of Other Items	
$700		
$800		
$900	Bootcamp	
$1000	Your Whole Enchilada	

OTHER PRODUCTS:
eBooks, CDroms
Audios, Videos
Seminars, Bootcamps
Teleseminars
(www.telephonebridgesavers.com)

SPEAKING ENGAGEMENTS (www.speeking.com) $$$$$$$$$$$$$$$$$ HIGH END CONSULTING (www.consultingexpert.com)

Your Holy Grail: Capture the Greatest Number of Opt-In Emails

YOU Can Make DOUBLE or TRIPLE What the Average Author/Speaker/Consultant Makes!

© Fred Gleeck 2001
Fred Gleeck Productions • 1-800-FGLEECK • 209 Horizon Peak Drive • Henderson, NV 89012 • fgleeck@aol.com
(Graphic layout by Ken Robertson Productions 904-806-3193)

Take a look at the graphic above. At the top of this funnel you need to put leads into our funnel system and as people come out of the funnel, you need to create a line of products at different price points. These price points on your product/service "offerings" should range anywhere from $10 to $1,000. And eventually, even higher.

To collect your free gift, worth $97, send an email to tips@SellingInfoProducts.com

For a moment, forget about how you're going to get people into the funnel. Let's concentrate on the products and the price points in that funnel. What can you produce for under $10? Preferably a report delivered in PDF format.

Next will be a book. Your book will run between $10 to $30. Most books cost around that much.

At the $50 level, one option might be a two audiocassette (or CD-rom) program together. (Although audiocassettes are becoming more out of date because of the advent of CD ROMs, they still are used extensively and selling in the information products industry.)

A $100 item might be a digitally delivered monthly newsletter or an introductory 1/2 hour consultation. Again, these are only suggestions. You can come up with your own product at this or any of the price points. Just be careful not to UNDERPRICE your intellectual property. This is the single biggest mistake I see most info product marketers make.

At the $200 level, your product may be a seminar. What length? It depends on the price sensitivity of your niche.

By the way, you don't necessarily have to have just one product at each price point. You may have different products at each point. You may also create a product at a price between these price points. For example, although off-the-shelf videos at a Costco or other discount warehouse goes for $29 or $39, you may price your videos at $79 or $99, or in some cases, $195. The price points here are sort of arbitrary to get you thinking along a price continuum.

A $300 product might be some sort of a home study course and include an audio, a video and perhaps a workbook.

From this point upward (in price, but downward in the funnel), you will create a line of products that go anywhere from $400 to $1,000. Make sure they include different modalities of learning. Examples of things other than books, audios and videos might be: personal coaching, consulting, telseminars or bootcamps.

Coaching is a one-on- one consultation that you provide to a single individual. Consulting is when you work with an organization or institution to give them ideas that they can use to improve their businesses. Bootcamps are an extended multi-day seminar). These might run $1,000, $2,000, or even $10,000.

Many people want to know if an economic slowdown makes you need to adjust your price points downward. Through the ups and downs of the economy over the last 20 years, I have never seen any relationship between a downward turning economy and people NOT buying good information products. In fact, during the last economic hiccup I actually raised MY prices.

TIP: Think price points, not products, to begin with

Reports (both physical and e-delivered)

Reports will be your lowest priced products. Reports can be delivered physically, i.e. sent in the mail, or digitally, such as in PDF format, via email. In the past, many people would produce physical reports. Given today's online world, I'd recommend only having your reports available in a downloadable format. To physically print, address, stamp and ship out these reports would be costly and tough to justify for the amount of time involved.

PDF is a method of electronically delivering written material so that any computer can read it. Let me repeat that. The PDF format, developed by Adobe (www.adobe.com), produces a finished product that can be read by any computer. For those of us who are Mac owners, that's reassuring!

PDF works by taking a picture of your document and storing it in a very efficient way so that when it is transferred to another computer it remains in a readable format. It is not "platform dependent", which means it doesn't have to be a Mac, or an IBM or any other type of system. In other words, PDF is a software application that allows your computer to open and display a document such as a Microsoft Word file (or virtually any other file). The actual creation of your reports in a PDF format is simple. Trust me on that one. If you don't know how to do it, you'll be amazed at how easy it will be.

This has become the easiest and fastest way of distributing information to people via the internet, because it doesn't matter what type of computer they are using; you can be sure that they'll see your document or report or newsletter as you originally designed it.

These reports should be priced at somewhere under $10 - generally anywhere from $5 to $10. They should be fewer than 10 pages in length – ideally between five and seven pages. There is no specific length that's required, but you want to make sure that people feel that they have gotten their money's worth without giving away the store.

In these reports, you want to give very detailed and concentrated information that can be immediately utilized. These reports should be very specific in helping people accomplish one particular task. There should be very little fluff. Only include information that will be helpful in getting people to do what your report claims. Reports need to have information that is immediately usable to the consumer, can be written in a short form, and is very specific.

And at the end of each report, you're going to have a little box called a RESOURCE BOX. This resource box will provide them with more information enticing them to buy something more expensive off your product ladder. Here's an example of a good resource box:

Fred Gleeck is the world's top expert on seminars and seminar marketing. He has done close to 1400 one-day events over the past 20 years. His book, *Marketing and Promoting Your Own Seminars and Workshops* is a consistent best-seller in it's category. Twice a year he does his seminar on seminars (www.seminaronseminars.com). To receive his 7-day e-course (normally $37) on marketing and promoting your own seminars send a blank email to tips@seminarexpert.com. You can also contact him at 1-800-FGLEECK or fred@fredgleeck.com.

To get regular email tips on professional speaking, send an email to tips@professionalspeakingsuccess.com.

If you're interested in doing your own seminars and workshops, go to www.seminarexpert.com.

The main purpose of this resource box is to serve as an up-sell for your additional products and services. But remember, unless you provide them with a ton of value in the initial report, they won't think of buying anything else from you, so make the report worth their while.

There are two kinds of offers you can make in your resource box. In the example above I've chosen to make a "soft" offer. This is an offer to capture someone's name first rather than trying to sell them something right off the bat. What's the proper way to do it? There is no answer that I can give you except to TEST!

With your reports that people pay for, you already have their contact information so you don't need to make a soft offer. The only purpose of a soft offer is to capture a person's email address, which you already have if you sold them something already. Soft offers are generally made when you provide a report at no charge. People might use your report in an e-zine and your "payment" is the ability to capture email addresses of people who read the report and thus respond to the resource box.

If you price your report at $10, make sure to deliver much more than $10 worth of information. Every time you deliver a product or service to your customers, you need to give them ten times the value that they paid. If you do, they'll be back. And, they won't return your products. Everything you create should have a lifetime guarantee; therefore, you want to create products that don't get returned!

Let me give you an example of a report. Let's say you had a book with 25 chapters. You could create 20 or 30 different reports that take each one of the chapters in your book, generate a more detailed discussion and be targeted even more specifically to a particular area. Even the book topics would be of a more general nature, a report based on one of the chapters could be aimed at a very specific audience. Then, with a few changes, you could create a similar report aimed at another very specific audience. You may want to use the outline for your book, which we're going to talk about later, to create those reports. You can also bundle your reports in a variety of different ways to encourage people to buy more than one at a time.

Make sure that you do not make people feel ripped off if they buy both your reports AND your book.

Here's an example report I did called "How to Make $10,000 attending a $5,000 Seminar."

"How to Attend Any Seminar for Free and in Fact Make $10,000 (or more) Every Time You Attend an Event (even when you're not a speaker)"

How would you like to attend a $5,000 seminar and come back home from the event with $8,000 in your pocket?

It's possible, but you must have a SYSTEM. A system that's been tested. A system that works!

To make this happen you first must have a product or service to sell. You then want to try and find opportune times during the event to let people know about you and what you're selling.

In some instances you'll be able to sell your product or service on the spot. If you can, then by all means do it! If you can't, you'll

---

want to generate a boatload of well-qualified, HOT leads.

In most cases, you'll probably have to be satisfied with generating leads, but your individual situation may be different.

The difference usually revolves around the price point of the product/service that you're selling. What's the RIGHT price point? It depends. Bad answer, but true.

You'll generate these leads by asking the RIGHT questions and making the RIGHT comments at events.

When people come over to you as the result of you asking or answering a question, be prepared to "hold court."

As people come up to you, start a circle going with you in the center. Try and move your group into a quiet area where you don't have to scream to have everyone hear you.

Where Should You Sit at Events?

Always sit at one of the four corners of a room. This means you will sit on the front row either all the way on the left or all the way on the right. Another option would be to sit on the back row on the far left and right.

I actually PREFER to sit in the back row on the right. I don't think this is necessarily THE best place because people have to turn around to look at you. Most people would say that the front row either left or right would be the best.

Frankly, I choose that location because it allows me to slip out easier if the speaker is terminally boring.

The reason for choosing these locations is simple. They are the only locations in the room where you can be easily seen by everyone in the room. When you stand (which you always should) to make a comment, everyone in the room will be able to see who you are.

Strategic Comments/Question Asking

There are two times where you can highlight yourself at your seminar. One is where you make comments. The other is where you ask questions.

Comments:

Make comments at a seminar when you have something VALU-ABLE to contribute. When you do it, it should not APPEAR to be self-promotional. It should APPEAR to be giving people valuable information.

If you're doing it right, you will be giving people great information, BUT, you'll also be promoting yourself!

Here's an example from a recent event.

I was at a recent marketing seminar where the speaker was discussing an internet issue. I then spoke up and told people about a VERY important issue that few people know about. When I made my comment everyone came up to me at the next break to ask me for more information about that topic.

There's a specific method for answering questions at a seminar or event. Every answer has got to show people how bright and insightful you are AND make them want to come up to you at the next break.

At another event, I made this comment:

"In my testing I've discovered that reserving certain key misspellings within your topic makes sense. Since I do a lot of work with professional speakers, I own the site: www.speeking.com. This site gets over 200 unique visitors and closes over 5% of those individuals on a $100 front end product."

This comment accomplished two things. First, it gave people a GREAT concept they can use for themselves AND it promoted my site: www.speeking.com. That's the kind of comment you want to make.

Questions:

The way you ASK a question is critical. Before you ask a concise, highly intelligent question you've got to precede the question with a mini-bio.

In your mini-bio you want to show people that you have a lot on the ball in your specific area.

Here's an example: "I own over 100 websites, all of which make money selling a specific information product, what I'd like to know is blah, blah . . .?"

Never ask TOO MANY questions during an event. You'll be perceived as a pest. Hold your fire until you see the RIGHT opportunity, then take it.

Whenever people ask me about how many comments/questions constitutes too many, I tell them my rule of thumb is NO MORE than 3 per day.

Preparation

Before you go to an event, you've got to have your ducks in a row. You should have a list of self-promotional items to make sure and bring to every event.

I forgot to bring all of the items listed below at a recent event and lost thousands of dollars.

Here's my list: 1-page order sheet; copies of all of my books; flyer promoting any and all upcoming events; flyer promoting any soon to be released products; articles by or about you.

Come with all of the above and you'll be armed for the battle.

What to Wear

Whenever I go to a seminar and event I wear my "Coogi" sweaters. These are extremely bright (and many people feel obnoxious) multi-colored sweaters. These have become my trademark. In fact, I'm known as "The Sweater Guy."

To give you a complete idea of the look that I use, I'm either in a pair of jeans or a nice pair of dress slacks. The only thing I don't like is wearing uncomfortable shoes which are the only kind I have that match my dress slacks. I prefer jeans!

I'm not suggesting you do the sweater thing, but I AM suggesting that you wear something that will make you stand out from the crowd. That way, people will remember you.

I'm not suggesting that you dress up in a clown outfit. Keep it memorable, but keep it professional. People should be able to spot you easily at one of the breaks.

What You SHOULDN'T Do

Don't become a pest or annoyance at any event. There is nothing worse than someone who over-contributes at events. People start to get annoyed. Pick your times and issues carefully. Only comment or ask questions when it DIRECTLY relates to you and/or your field of expertise.

This would mean a maximum of 3 instances during the day when you speak. This seems to be the most anyone should contribute in the course of an event.

Question the Status Quo

Look for ways to be different from anyone at the events. To stand out, but to stand out in a positive way.

No one cares if all you're going to do is agree with the speaker with your comments. That will bring a HUGE YAWN regardless of how articulate you are in making your point.

Questions peoples assumptions and "sacred cows" but do so in an intelligent, articulate, manner. Also make sure and do it in a way that doesn't directly challenge the speaker and make them look bad.

Printed Matter

Whatever it is you're trying to promote should have a flyer or other printed matter associated with them.

At a recent seminar that I attended I was hoping to promote a series of seminars that I was going to have in the upcoming months.

I printed up a one page sheet with a list of the seminars and some bullet points associated with each seminar. I included all of the websites associated with each of the seminars. Someone won't be sold with a one page flyer but they are much more apt to buy at a website.

Don't try and promote more than one thing or one set of things.

For example, I wouldn't want to try and promote both my seminars AND a whole set of my products.

Your Book

People tell you to bring business cards to events that you attend. That's OK, but there's something MUCH better. Bring a copy of your book!

Don't have a book? Write one or get one written.

If you need more information on how to do this, go to www.self-publishingsuccess.com.

A book will give you a massive amount of credibility in any marketplace. It's infinitely better than a business card.

What topic should your book be about? Preferably in the field that you want to "hold court." That would be the best, but a book in ANY related topic will do.

By handing out my books I end up getting three things:

Orders for books, people onto my opt-in lists and orders for my other programs that are listed in the back of the book on the order sheets.

Get the Mike!

At many seminars and events, they pass a mike around for people to ask questions. He/she who controls the mike, wins!

Get a hold of the mike in advance of making a comment or asking a question. When there is a gap in the action, shoot.

Don't interrupt anyone, but when there is a gap, jump in!

The Kind of Events You Attend

Unless you attend the right kind of events, this system WILL NOT WORK! What's the "right" type of event? One where you have a match with your product or service offering. This means that if you sell civil war memorabilia you don't want to go to internet marketing seminars. There's just NOT a match!

This doesn't mean that you should only attend seminars attended by your peers. Attend events where your peers are there only to learn more about your business and socialize. If you're trying to attend events for the PURPOSE of selling your products and services, look for events where your PROSPECTS will be in attendance.

Your Contact Info

My 800 number is 1-800-FGLEECK. I've had this 800 number for 18 years. An 800 number is better than an 888, an 877 or an 866. Why? The 800 number shows you've been around a lot longer. Even if you get one today (which is tough to do), people will still associate longevity with your business if you have an 800 number.

I like to have my email match my 800 number so my email address is fgleeck@aol.com. I suggest YOU do the same.

If you CAN'T find an 800 number, go ahead and get either an 888, 877 or 866 number in that that order. If possible, try to make it a "vanity" number. One where the numbers spell something out as well.

Conclusion

Seminars that you attend are the best lead generation and sales opportunity on the planet. Go to events and follow the suggestions mentioned above and you'll be able to make MUCH MORE than the cost of the seminars that you attend. Good luck and good hunting!

To receive Fred's 7-day course (normally $37) *FREE on Marketing and Promoting Your Own Seminars and Workshops* send an email to tips@seminarexpert.com

YOUR BOOK

Book Basics

The next item on the price point list is a book. Your book. This section is a brief overview on how to write and create your own book. For more information on this topic, you can purchase my e-book entitled "Publishing for Maximum Profit" at www.publishingbook.com. Either that, or visit my site: www.selfpublishingsuccess.com where you'll find my one-day seminar on audio covering the self publishing process. Your book is one of your least expensive yet hardest to create products, but it is your most important one. Notice that I didn't attempt to sell you a physical copy of my book directly. I only fulfill orders for over $100 directly through my own office. I suggest you do the same. People who want JUST your physical books, send them to Amazon if the total order is under $100.

Why is a book the most important item on your list? A book can get you on a radio talk show. Audio programs will not. People don't care about audio programs. They don't care about videos. They don't care about written reports. They don't perceive these items as worthy of press or publicity. They are all information products that make you a lot of money, but they are not credibility builders. You need to have a physical book. Your book is crucial. Your book is the key. Your book is the BEST business card you can ever create. It' the ultimate credibility builder.

It is also one of the BEST ways to generate "opt-in" names for your list. Here's how. People buy my books on amazon. In the book I "bribe" them to give me their email address in exchange for a valuable digital bonus. A large percentage of them then go to my site, sign up with their email addresses and get their freebie. I get their email address and can market to them forever. Good deal. Make sure you do the same. More about Amazon later.

If writing a book is the key to success, then why doesn't everyone write a book? The number one reason is perfectionism - just as with other aspects of information product creation. Another reason is a lack of understanding of the process. And lastly, there is the "imposter syndrome". People say to themselves "Who me? Write a book?" How many times have you seen someone on a talk show discussing their latest book and said to yourself, "I could've written that book."? Guess what? You could have. Difference? They did it!

There are a lot of topics out there that you know about and could write about. I will also let you in on a little secret. That person you saw on the talk show most likely felt the same way you are feeling now, but wrote a book anyway!

In order to create a book:
1. You need to research it
2. You need to write it
3. You need to print it
4. You need to sell it
5. You need to back end it

This means that before you start writing the book, you need to do your homework. You need to conduct research and gather as much data as possible. Don't worry if and where you'll use the information, just get as much of it as you can immediately. After you've gathered all the data I suggest you put together a very specific outline. I always recommend the 25 x 4 x 2 system. In this system you create 25 major chapter headings, 4 sub-headings under each chapter, and then write 2 pages for each sub-heading. That is my standard template and will create you a 200-page book.

I've also found that some of my clients seem to work very well using the "index card" system. This is where you take all of the major topics (chapter headings) and place them each on an individual index card. Then you write the subheadings underneath the heading you put on every index card. Don't try and do them in order, this will hurt your brainstorming process. On each card write any stories, quotes or statistics that you can use to support your points. When you finally start writing, this system will make it a lot easier for you.

After writing your book, make sure to get someone to edit it for you. You can NOT effectively edit your own work. This is something you MUST have done. Where do you find an editor? Check out my Million Dollar Rolodex at www.TheProductGuru.com to get my latest recommendations.

Once you've researched it, created the outline and written it, you need to create both "bounce back" and "back end" offers. Bounce back offers are very blatant, free offers for digital products or reports. This is where you try and get people to send for your free digital report if they give you their email address. Even if it's free, you'll still need to sell people on responding. People get so much "junk" in their email boxes that you will still need to SELL them on getting it.

My friend, Mike Litman came up with a brilliant way to bounce people back from his book. He put a solicitation on the bottom of every page to get people to get something at no charge. In addition to promoting your e-reports on the bottom of every page, you'll also want to put two more things in your books to get people to bounce-back to you. You'll need to put a full page ad in the front and back of your book. Another bounceback should be imbedded in the text of your book.

In my book "Publishing for Maximum Profit" I bounce people back to a 7-day e-course. I tell them that if they send a blank email to tips@selfpublishingsuccess.com I'll send them a 7-day e-course for free that is normally worth $37.

If you want to get a free report on this, or other topics, send an e-mail to tips@seminarexpert.com. And by the way, if you go to send an e-mail to tips@seminarexpert.com you will automatically be enrolled into a series of auto responders, which we'll talk about later.

Bounce back offers are important for two reasons. One is a very direct reason. If someone buys your book by calling up on the phone, you will send the book AND have the name of the customer in the database. Any bounce back offers will be used to up-sell – you now have them in your funnel and you can get them to buy bigger and more expensive products.

The other reason is far more indirect. If you were to buy 100 copies of my book and sell them at your seminars, I am not going to know who the buyers of those books are. The same is true if the book sells through a book club. Therefore, I need to create a way to capture the names of the people who have my book that did not get the book directly from me. My bounce back offers give me a chance to collect their name and email and get them into my funnel and trade them up the ladder.

Another indirect way for people to acquire my book is through what I call "reverse shoplifting". I will go into bookstores and I will leave one of my books on the shelf. This costs me about $3. Why would I want to go into a bookstore and leave a book on the shelf? If you were browsing in Borders and found my book and decided to buy it, you would take it up front. The $7 per hour clerk will scan it and, of course, nothing will come up. The clerk will undoubtedly call over the manager who will say, "Take the money and we'll worry about the scan later."

This means that someone buys my book and I don't get any money for it. In fact, I have actually paid $2.80 for them to get my book. I have determined, however, that if only one out of ten that buys my book in this method decides to buy something else due to the bounce back offers, then I am making money and have found a great and cheap method of marketing.

And then, a year or so from now, I will call Borders and say, "By the way, you've been selling my book but you haven't known it. Take a look at the record at Store #459 and you'll see my ISBN number that they have been selling. I've been putting my book on your shelf and it's been selling really well. Now I think you should actually start buying them from me." The books are the key to making it happen.

The back-end offer is to get people who buy the book to buy a more expensive item, like an audio program on a related product. Check the back of this book to see what I suggest you do. Give people much more than you promised them with your book and they will be highly likely to buy other things that you offer.

Book Printing

Once you have the book written and the bounce back and back end offers in place, you need to think about the printing. I have a very strong rule when it comes to your first run: Never produce more than 100 books the first time out. Why? There are two main reasons. The first is to keep your expenses down. You don't want to have a lot of money tied up in inventory before you start making some money. The second reason is that there will be mistakes in it the first time around. Your customers will often find these mistakes and you can correct them before you go into bigger production. My usual printing progression is 100 copies for the first run, 500 copies for the next run, 1,000 copies on the third run and from that point, the printing should be based upon the demand.

Let me repeat my rule again. I don't care how good you think the book is, or how perfect you find it, do not EVER print more than 1,000 copies, preferably not more than 100, for the first run. Pay the additional unit cost; do not have your entire garage stocked with inventory. I have heard countless stories from many different people - countless nightmares of books sitting there for years. Don't do it. I don't care how good a deal they offer you. Now, if your book becomes a best seller over night, fine. Then you can turn around and do another printing really quickly. But for your first run of books, follow the 100, 500, 1000 routine.

Look in my Million Dollar Rolodex at the back of this book for a reference on who I use for printing. Or you can establish your own relationship with a Print-on-Demand or short run book printer. You'll also want to check the site: www.TheProductGuru.com which always has the most recent version of all of my contacts listed.

Let me warn you up front about the folks in the POD market. Almost everyone I've ever used has gone bankrupt. The service is universally weak and the quality of the product they will produce is OK at best. But, you should still do it. The book they'll print for you will be better than no book at all and the quality although imperfect, will be adequate.

Once you start producing more than 1000 books, you will have to use someone other than a Print on Demand printer. More than 1000 copies, you will want to find a "short run" book printer. Your cost per unit will be much lower with a short run printer. When you move from POD printers into short run book publishing, you need to look at efficiency. The typical short run order is between 1000 and 3000 copies – otherwise, it's not cost effective. Let me give you some pricing just to give you an idea.

A 200-page book with a nice 4-color cover that looks like a Barnes and Noble book will cost between five and six dollars per book for 100 copies. Now, if you go to 500 copies, the price might drop to $3.50. And if you go to 1,000 copies, the price might drop to $2.75. So, you have prices that range all the way from $2.75 up to about six dollars, depending on quantity. Well, again, why produce just 100?

First off, you don't know how many you're going to sell and I don't want you to have a whole lot sitting around in your garage or basement or warehouse or wherever it is. So I don't want you to produce a lot at one time.

The second thing is that we want your customers to correct the book for you. In the first run, most of your errors are going to be corrected. So in the first 100 copies, you're going to tell people "By the way, if you find any errors, send them to me." And usually when I do this I even offer some kind of a gift. I say "If you find more then ten typos in my book, I will send you a free gift." This gets people to meticulously comb through your books to find every single possible mistake. There are some really anal-retentive people out there that will do it!! You get your customers to do the editing for you! Your second run will be significantly better in terms of error count, and by the third run, your book will be virtually clean.

ISBN Number

Before you get your ISBN numbers, you will want to set up your publishing house. Be sure not to use your own name as the publishing business – this looks too amateurish. The name of my publishing company is Fast Forward Press. I got that in a fit of brilliance sitting there looking at my audio tape recorder. I said to myself "Press Fast Forward" and I said "No. Fast Forward Press". I use two arrows as the logo.

I don't really care what you name your company but it shouldn't have your name in it. You want to use something generic that would allow you to move from niche to niche without having to change publishing companies. So if you called it Karate Press it wouldn't work if you changed niches because it's so specific. Keep it generic. Look at Random House! Fast Forward Press is generic enough that I can use it for a lot of different niches.

To set up a publishing company you can either set it up as a sole proprietorship or incorporate. I don't want to give you legal advice, but the first option is much less expensive. All it involves in most cities is to file a "ficticious name" form with your county. This will allow you to open up a checking account in the name of your new publishing house.

Once you set up your publishing company name, you need to get a set of ISBN numbers. Go to bowker.com you can find them at: www.bowker.com.

ISBN numbers are the social security numbers for each of your products, including your books. Each product should be assigned a separate ISBN number. You'll need them when you start selling books and other products. As set of 10 ISBN numbers will run around $350.

You do not have to change your ISBN when you make minor changes to your book. If you make revisions or add chapters or simply make corrections, the ISBN number remains the same. It is your book and you can do anything you want to it. If you did a major revision, you may have to label the book as a "Revised Edition", but you will maintain the same ISBN and the same copyright.

Cover/Interior Design

While you are writing the book, (in Microsoft Word format – the most accepted format) you should be getting your cover created by a cover designer. It makes sense to design a nice cover. I used to think that it wasn't worth it to spend the money on a good cover since most of the books would not be sold in a bookstore. I am now convinced that it is well worth spending the money. Cover Design is crucial. People don't judge a book by its cover – or so the old expression says. NOT TRUE. This is the one area you should not scrimp on. People do judge a book by its cover. BUT, if the content stinks, it won't matter.

Make sure to hire a professional cover designer to help you in this area. The one I recommend is Nick Zelinger of NZ Graphics. He is an experienced and affordable designer and producer of covers and books. Look him up in the Million Dollar Rolodex in the back of the book.

I also recommend Tami Dever. She is listed in the Million Dollar Rolodex in the back of the book.

In order to use a POD printer, the cover size should be 5-1/2 by 8-1/2. You can get them bigger, but it will cost you more. The reason is simple: A 5-1/2 by 8-1/2 is an 8-1/2 by 11 sheet of paper folded in half (slightly less due to trimming) and that's going to cost you a lot less money than creating a larger-sized cover.

If you eventually get your book into bookstores, you may decide to use a slightly larger size of book. Don't worry about that for right now. You can still sell your book through bookstores at the smaller size I suggest above.

How much will it cost to design a good cover? It will cost between $1,200 and 1,500 to get one designed by a pro. I'm willing to spend the $1,200 to $1,500 because the book is part of your image. Once you have a book, you are considered an expert in the field. If my book looks professional, then I am considered even more qualified. Remember that your book becomes your best piece of promotional material.

A book as a business card? How so? Let me give you a personal example. I was sitting on a plane and struck up a conversation with the person seated next to me. I asked him what he did. He told me and then asked me the same question. I said, "Well, I'm a consultant. I'm a marketing consultant." He said, "Oh, do you have a card?" I said "No, I don't, but would you like a copy of my book?" Do you know what he replied to that? "Your book? Oh my God, you're an author". It's unbelievable. Having a book elevates you to expert status. It also will make you much more confident when you go out there and sell your products. Additionally, it will increase your ability to get speaking engagements, radio shows, media reviews, etc.

I mentioned that you would want a book with a 4-color cover. A four-color cover just means that it's not a black and white cover. With a four-color process, four different colors, cyan, magenta, black and yellow, all work together. All four of these colors together make every color in the rainbow. Therefore, four-color means the ability to print any kind of color, whatsoever. If it were a two-color process, it would just mean printing black ink on a blue cover, red ink on a white cover, etc.

Once the book is written and your cover designer has finished designing the cover, the designer will then do what's called the interior design. This is a fancy way of saying that they make the book look pretty on the page and match the cover. For example, if you notice the typestyle that was used on the cover of this book, you will see that the chapter headings also employ a similar typestyle that was used to create a consistency between the outside and the inside of the book. This was done by the people who did my cover and interior design. They take it and make it ready to send to the printers of the world, usually in a PDF format.

In order to be ready for the printer, the manuscript has to have all sorts of things: proper margins, appropriate typeface, where to put the chapter headings and sub-headings, lines or borders, etc. Even if you are a technical person, you should not be concentrating on these things. Leave it to the professionals. Let your cover designers and the interior designers and the editors to take your printed information, make it look pretty on the page, design you a great cover, and deliver it to the printer. Whatever your curiosity about the process, although an interesting exercise, you don't need to spend your time worrying about the production of your book. You need to spend time creating products, not obsessing about that minutiae.

So, the book is written, the bounce back offers are in place, the cover is designed, and the interior is ready to go. It is time for the printer. The older way of doing things was to take your manuscript to a printer and they generate a book – no PDF involved. With the newer technology, however, this is no longer an efficient way to get things done. It also creates a lower print quality. Why? If I am a printer doing things the old way, I have to take the printed page that you give me and take a photograph of it, create what's called a "plate", and then start making copies. With the PDF process, we eliminate the need for the plate and go directly, digitally, from the version given by the interior design folks to the printer. This not only increases quality, but cuts time and cost as well.

Remember, however, that you don't have to worry about it! You write your book in Microsoft Word, you send it to Tami (the designer), she does the cover, they do the interior, they give it to the printer, and you're out of the picture. They send you some copies before they're done, but you don't have to mess with all the printing details. Spend that time creating other products that will earn you money!

Is there ever a time that you would want to sell out to a major publisher like Warner Books? The answer is probably yes, but nowhere in the near future. Perhaps after you have six, or eight or ten titles under your belt. Then you might go to a Warner Books or a John Wiley or someone like that and say "Hey. Would you like to give me a million and a half dollars to start carrying these titles?"

There is one condition on this, however. I will never go to a major publisher (or suggest that you do) and give them the rights to my books unless they guarantee me that they will allow me to keep my bounce back offers in the book. That's the only thing I care about. The bounce back offers allow people to get in touch with me, both in the text itself and in the back. And this becomes a big bone of contention to the publishers because they legitimately see that they may be losing out on some of the sales through bookstores and traditional channels. That to me becomes a non-starter in the contract negotiation if they will not agree to allow the bounce back offers to remain. If they will agree to the bounce back offers, I personally would love to have all my books distributed by a large book company. But the problem is trying to get a large publishing house to take your book. It is virtually impossible because they're such arrogant S.O.B.s.

NOT true of one distributor, who has agreed to work with me to get my books into bookstores. There name is Midpoint Trade and I highly recommend them. He MAY be able to help you as well. Your contact there is Eric Kampmann. I suggest you give Eric a call. Don't be surprised if your book or topic is NOT appropriate for them as a company, but it's worth a shot. He can be reached at: 212-727-0190.

I would highly recommend that you buy my self-publishing course. It will give you a lot MORE useful and helpful information. Take a look at www.selfpublishingsuccess.com. Or pick up a copy of my e-book at www.publishingbook.com.

Authors who don't know any better try and make money from their books. If you do, consider it a bonus. Many people have probably attended the same seminars that I have. They've been taught the old and outdated model of trying to get your books in the bookstores and then sell a bunch of copies. It's great to have your book for sale in the big bookstores, but this is not where the big money is made. The big money is made with all of the products and services you sell to people AFTER they buy your book.

If you like any of my books, you can call my printer directly and order as many copies as you want at cost, and sell them yourself at retail price. What that means is you can buy this book or any of my books and then sell them at full retail. You'll only pay whatever my printer charges you plus shipping. Depending on how many you order they will run you between about $3 and $5 a piece.

Now, why the heck would I want to do this? Because I don't care about my book making money. I only care about my book getting my name out in the market place and serving as the front end to my process, to drive people back into my funnel, to trade them up to higher and higher price point products. This is my model. I'm not saying this is the only model. It is my model; it's the model I am suggesting you consider because it certainly does make a lot of sense. And it works for me.

E-books

What is an e-Book? It is simply a book in electronic format. E-books are great. Once you write them, your cost of goods is virtually zero. This means that you don't have to sell a whole lot of them to make money. So, how do you create an e-book?

Take your existing book and add some bonuses to it and justify the higher price you charge. Typically, a physical book of mine will sell for between \$15 and \$20. My ebooks sell for about double that price. You normally charge more for your ebook than your physical book. For example, I took my book Marketing and Promoting Seminars and Workshops, produced it in e-Book form, and then I sold it. I don't want to be selling something as an e-book for less than \$29 or \$39, so how do I justify the difference in price between \$14.95 for the print version and \$29 or \$39.95 or whatever I sell it for as an e-Book? I justify it by giving people other kinds of bonuses. I give them a free digital bonus or two and some discounts off some of my other products and services. This helps to justify the increased price.

A lot of people, by the way, who buy the e-book, then want the physical book. Why? I don't know ... they just like to have a physical book sitting on their shelf. I understand that: I prefer a physical book to an e-Book, but lots of people want to get the book right now and if they're online they will buy it in an e-Book form.

Here are some examples of bonuses I use:

- Attend my next seminar at 50% off if you buy this e-Book
- Attend a free tele-seminar, normally \$49, yours free when you buy today
- A 15 minute free consultation over the phone
- A critique coupon allowing them to send something into me that I will give comments on and send back to them.

There are lots of different possible bonuses but, again, my suggestion would be to offer bonuses that don't cost you any out of pocket time or money.

I mentioned to you earlier about creating a bounce back offer within the text of your book in multiple places. You will also want to include bounce back offers within your e-book text and on the front and the back ends. So that means for your e-book, as well as your physical book, you want to have a big page on the front and a big page on the back that says "Free Offer". It just shouts "Look at this page!" because again, what we're doing is getting those people who bought from indirect channels to see this free offer. We want them to say "Wow! I want to get that free offer".

TIP: Even if you're giving something away for free you have to sell it.

You should be doing everything you possibly can to capture the names of the people who bought through indirect channels (either your book or your e-Book,) or who stole your e-Book because it's in PDF format. The PDF format will allow you to copy and as far as I'm concerned, I hope there are thousands, hundreds of thousands of copies of my book running around all over the web as long as it's intact. If it is intact, my bounce back offers will get people coming back to me and I won't even know where they're from!

For a while, I gave away copies of my book Publishing for Maximum Profit on the web. I hope that people are copying it and sending it to friends. I want them to. Why? Because it creates sales on my bounce back offers AND it also makes me known to a wider audience. All of a sudden, I'm out there and getting more well-known by the minute. A very, very powerful concept.

Even when you have a good front end and back end bounce back offer, and a lot of content in your e-Book, only about 20% will take you up on your offer. If you can present a really good offer, 20% of the people who bought the book through indirect channels might get back with you. Don't be disappointed by this number. It takes a lot of effort to motivate anyone to do anything. If you're getting that more than 20% of people to take you up on your bounceback offer, you're doing a great job.

You will also want to create e-links within the book and use all of the functions of an e-book. Within a PDF formatted book that you're digitally delivering within the Adobe Acrobat system, it creates what are called hyper links. This means within the text of the book there are clickable links that take you to places. So within the book, if I put www.seminarexpert.com within the text of the link, they can click on it and they go via Internet Explorer or Netscape or whatever they're using, right into my web site. It's a great way to get people to investigate your entire product line.

You can also use hyper links for other people's products. It might be for products in which you created an affiliate relationship. An affiliate relationship is when you get paid to sell someone else's stuff through a program where you create a link that has your code on it.

Let me give you an example. Let's say that I sign up for a friend's affiliate program through their website and they agree to give me 50% of everything I sell. I put his product in my e-book. When somebody clicks on my affiliate link they will go to that person's website. If they buy something, now or in the future, I'll get the credit for it and a check. This person is paying for me to send business his way.

Affiliates are a great system. This gives you the opportunity to find people in a similar field and rather than be competitors, you can be collaborators. If you were to sit down with these affiliates and discuss philosophies, they might be entirely different than your own. But chances are, your customers, once they've read your stuff and absorbed all your material, are going to want to go on to the next guru. People devour of one person's material, they get hot about the topic, and then they buy the next person's stuff. There is no need to think of this as competition. It's a big world out there. Cooperation rather than competition is another key to success in the information products business.

An e-Book does NOT replace a physical book, and a physical book does not replace an e-Book. You need both in your price point structure!

A final note: Please do NOT skimp on your e-Book cover. It makes sense to design a nice cover for an e-book just like for a physical book. I suggest you go to www.elance.com or visit my friend Armand Morin's site: www.ebookcovergenerator.com!

If you want to look at some of my examples of ebook sites that I've done, take a look at:

www.publishingbook.com
www.seminarguru.com
www.sellingproductsfromtheplatform.com
www.speakingformillions.com

All of these are examples of exactly how you should be promoting your ebooks.

AUDio PROGRaMS

The Process

Remember earlier when I talked about modalities of learning? People who buy books like to read. That's their primary modality of learning. Another modality is audio and can be delivered in the audiotape, CDrom, MP3, or downloadable audio form. Regardless of what form you put the audio in, there are only a limited number of ways for you to create the audio product.

- In-Studio: Solo (you record it on your own)
- In-Studio: Interview Style (you interview of get interviewed by someone)
- Live Seminar (you record a live event)
- Teleseminar or Telephone Interview (you record a live event over the phone)

In Studio - Solo

You can do what's called "in studio" where you sit down with a microphone in a studio and record a program. Those of you who have heard some of Tony Robbins programs, (Personal Power), know what I mean. He records his material sitting in an audio booth talking into a microphone without any help or assistance.

You could also record a program sitting in my living room alone. But do you know what? It would be really, really weak because there's no audience interaction. There's no energy that comes from people giving you feedback. This method doesn't work nearly as well as finding a way to get some audience interaction.

To be honest, this is how I did a couple of my very first audio programs. I sat down in the living room with a little radio shack mike and went through my outline as if I were explaining things to another interested party in the room. It was saleable, but not near-ly as good as it could have been.

If you are going to do it in studio, I would encourage you to not go solo, but to go with an interview style of recording. This is where I sit down with you and we record a product together. I do a lot of these interviews for my clients and if you want, you can always get in touch with me to discuss your individual needs. I really love doing audio interviews because I get to learn about a specific topic and I'm pretty good at it.

You give me an outline, I ask you questions, and I serve as sort of the naïve interviewer. Basically, I'm the advocate for your listener on tape. I'm asking you the questions that the listener would ask of you if they were there with you in person. So, it pays in a way to have someone there who doesn't really know a ton about the topic because that person can ask really good questions that the listener would prob-ably want asked and answered. Questions that you don't even think to come up with yourself!

In the interview style, you can do an in person interview or you can record one over the phone. You can either serve as the expert where you are the interviewee OR you can be the interviewer and get peo-ple to answer the questions that you ask. If you're not an expert in the topic, find others who are and interview them.

For instance, let's say that martial arts is your topic. One of things you might do is to talk to the twenty top martial artists in the country. You would ask them their philosophy and record it for 45 to 60 minutes. You can get these interviews for free. Why? You give them the right to give out their contact information, which allows them to fill their funnel. If you wanted to interview me on marketing, I'd be happy to do it. Why? You can sell it and I get my name out there for free. For 45 minutes of my time, you are now selling these tapes to people and I'm represented as an expert. It is a win – win proposition.

So, now you have interviewed the twenty top martial arts experts in the world. Make it sixteen, and that way you can package it in a nice binder that will hold 16 cassette tapes. So, now you've packaged the 16 cassette tapes of martial arts masters telling you their philosophy. It's a great product. What price point are we going to put on this product? I would sell it for at least $195 and more likely for $295.

Anyone reading this book can take their topic and interview the top people in the industry. You record their thoughts, duplicate them and get them into finished form. You have your product done almost immediately. This doesn't have to be a long, time-consuming process.

I recently spoke with someone who is a big shot – he's one of the voices on a VERY popular animated TV show. He's writing a book and he calls me up to help him make an audio recording of his book. I called him back and I said "You know, I don't know if you've noticed but you're missing the whole point here. If you just read your book into an audiocassette, that's going to be a $19.95 product. I want to create audio programs for you that sell for $99 or $199, not just you sitting there reading your book into a tape recorder. That makes no sense." Traditional publishers will do that. I don't encourage you to do it that way because you're not going to maximize the amount of money that you make.

Another way to record an audio program is to record a seminar. You have two choices for recording seminars: either large group format or small group format. In a small group format, I put the recording device on the desk. You ask a question, and I answer. It's recording everything that we're doing. That's how you do it in a small group setting such as a boardroom. I encourage you to record your audio-tapes of seminars in small groups if possible because to do it in large groups is really expensive and really dicey.

Why? If we had 300 people in a room, in order to get any kind of viable sound quality, what we'd have to do is have the audience miked up, and someone would have to go out there with the microphone. It's a royal pain in the butt. That's not to say that you should only have small seminars!! Please have 300 or 400 people in your seminar. But for the purposes of creating a recording, do it during a small group environment. Tape it this way and it's much more effective and efficient.

Editing isn't necessary. I don't do it. I don't recommend you do it. It takes away from the spontaneity of the event and I think that it just isn't necessary even if you're doing it in studio.

Others may disagree with me on this one, but that's how I feel.

The Equipment

Many people will rent equipment or hire people to do their audio programs. If you are serious about this business, and plan to create a fair amount of product, it pays to own your own equipment. If you're getting started on a shoestring, go down to Radio Shack and get some of your equipment from them. Just don't rent anything. You'll get overcharged. Also, remember not to skimp on a mike. No matter how average your recorder, get a "decent" mike.

For any professional quality recording devices, I would encourage you to go to Kingdom. They're in the Million Dollar Rolodex at the back of this book. They sell pretty much everything that you would need to buy when producing audio programs in either digital or analog form. They're a great source for everything audio. They are incredible in terms of their customer service. If you find something that you want that they don't have in their catalogue, ask them about it. They may be able to get a hold of the item.

Kingdom primarily serves the religious market, so every once in awhile you'll hear "… and what church are you calling from?" and you just tell them the Church of Massive Money Making and they'll be kind of quiet from then on! I think it's because of their work in the religious market that they've got such a great customer service orientation. I also think it's because of their CEO, a guy named Johnny Berguson. I've met him by phone and he's exceptionally good. Call Kingdom for a catalog. You can get a good recording device starting around $200.

Should you produce these audiotapes in digital format? I suggest you produce them in both analog and digital formats. Some people recommend that you do your recording exclusively in digital form. I STRONGLY disagree. I have NEVER seen a traditional audio tape recorder "crap out" during an important event. I can NOT say that about recording on a digital device or directly onto a computer.

The thing to remember is you're dealing with voice recording is that it isn't mandatory to be using the state of the art audio equipment when dealing with voice. You MUST use great equipment when you're dealing with music. As you start to make more money, spend more and invest in better equipment. But, to get started you don't have to break the bank. If you only record in analog (cassette tape), it's easy enough to convert to digital. You can pay others to do this for you or you can "feed" the audio into your computer and produce it yourself. There is inexpensive software that can help you do this. I suggest you take a look online and put in the words: "inexpensive audio software" and see what comes up. As a Mac user, I've been using Final Vinyl and a program called Peak.

Whenever I record any audio program I try and do it simultaneously on both cassette and digital format. I use a device that allow me to produce both an audio tape and a CDrom simultaneously. It's a recorder that's called a Tascam and Kingdom sells it for about $700. It's well worth it! Regardless of what you use, make sure and back-up everything that you record immediately after you do it. NOT doing this will cause you major nightmares.

This machine allows you to record an audio cassette and a CD at the same time using one piece of equipment. I also now own a high end digital recorder from Marantz that has removable memory. If I want to record to that device and a cassette player simultaneously, I must use something called a mixer.

If I'm doing an interview, for example, I take both my mike and my interviewees mike and feed it through the mixer. The purpose of the mixer is simple. It mixes the two audio tracks and makes them into one. The mixer also has multiple outputs allowing me to have one signal going into a cassette recorder and the other one going into my digital recorder. It may sound complicated, but it's really pretty simple. The folks at Kingdom will gladly "coach" you through the process if you just ask them. After all, they will be selling you the equipment.

When you get a little more sophisticated, talk to me about my latest and best reccomendation in this area.

The tape you used to record onto will become your master tape. Then you will create what is called a "sub master". Then you will take this and use it to create another, the next version, and put it away in the vault. That's saved. And you will make copies off of this sub master. Why do you do that? To preserve your master. In other words, you want to have the least number of passes or copies made off of the master so that the master can be preserved in the best possible form. If you are recording in a digital format, the quality of the recording might be a tad better. However, our ability to create a sub master quickly and easily would be hindered. Like I said, I now do both.

The most important thing in getting a high quality recording is a good microphone. Microphone prices go from $20 to $300 or more. When you start, stick with what you can afford. Over time, a good mike will be a great investment.

One of the big advantages to recording in a digital format is the quality will never deteriorate. That's why I suggest that if you do use audio cassettes to record your masters, make sure and make a digital copy of them immediately. The problem with cassette tapes for the purists out there is the tape hiss that inevitably comes with recording on cassette. A good cassette recorder will have less of this, but it will still exist. You'll still want to produce both for the time being.

That brings us to duplication. Should you use outsourcing duplication or in-house duplication? If you're doing your duplication in-house, it generally will cost you about one-third of the cost of outsourcing - once you've invested in the equipment. So, if you are thinking about duplicating out of house, remember that you're probably not going to get your margins. Remember, you're looking to get at least a 1 to 15 or a 1 to 20 ratio between cost and sales price. By sending out your audiocassette tapes for external duplication, you really end up in a situation where you are not able to take advantage of these great margins – which is an important aspect of why you're in the information marketing business in the first place.

Now, what I would suggest you do is initially get an inexpensive machine from Kingdom. Start with one of those one-to-one duplicators. Do it yourself. Then move up, as I did, to a more expensive unit. There are three or four different levels of duplicating machines. They go anywhere from a low of $199.00 up to a high of $1,500.00. I've got a $1,500.00 unit because of the volume I produce. It's a one-to-three model. You put one in and you make three, just like that. Occasionally you may need to get your equipment serviced, so realize that equipment isn't flawless. You can also burn your own CD's. Plenty of people have CD burners, so that's perfectly acceptable.

You will also need a phone jack for your recording device so that you can record tele-seminars and interviews right over the phone. Some recorders have them built in. For those that don't, you can go to the Radio Shack and pick up a small device that will allow your device to record via the phone. This allows you to create your product quickly and easily.

Other Formats

Should you put your recording into an MP3 format? Sure. I'd encourage you to sell your audio programs in any and every format that you can. With the prevalence of MP3 players you'll want to have it in every possible format INCLUDING MP3. Why not? It costs virtually nothing to do it.

Eventually, what's going to happen is that every piece of data that you have or own is going to be sitting on a hard drive of some sort in your house and you are going to be able to access it through PIN numbers from a remote system - whether traveling, with a walkman, with anything. In the meantime, however, we're going to deliver things to people over the web, they're going to download it and burn it onto a CD or some kind of a video or DVD, and be able to play it anywhere in their house. That's the interim step.

What's important to remember is that you're a content provider. Content is KING. As long as you have great content in audio form (even in analog format) you have information that is worth a bundle. If it's good!

Video

In addition to reading and listening, some people prefer to learn by watching. So you'll want to produce videos as part of your product arsenal. I had a guy at one of my coaching meeting who ONLY buys video. He said he would pay double or triple to price of an audio program to get the material in VHS or DVD form. He's not the average buyer, but why alienate someone and prevent them from spending big money with you?

You also might have something to sell people that REQUIRES a visual presentation to make sense. You couldn't teach people how to do Origami using an audio. With those things that require video you have no choice. Even in those cases where video isn't required, it's a good thing to have.
With a video product, you have two primary options. You can record a live event or you can produce a video using live actors with a script. A live event isn't scripted, of course, but you must have an outline.

If you do record a live event, always have backup equipment. I had a problem at an event not long ago. Luckily I was thinking right. I had brought a backup unit for my little DV recorder and my little DV camera. Thank goodness, because one of them pooped out on me! I used my spare and got the system up and running right away and it was perfect. If I had not had my backup with me, I would have been in serious trouble. I had already sold copies of the video for that seminar before the seminar was even produced!

Make sure you are using digital video. You can either buy your own equipment, rent it, or you can hire someone to do the whole thing for you. If you hire someone, generally look for someone who has a 3-chip DV camera.

There are two primary types of DV cameras. The first is a 1-chip, the second is a 3-chip. Another option is to use BetaCam equipment. That is professional quality equipment and these days, with good lighting doesn't look all that much better than a good 3 chip DV camera. Let me give you some of the ratios here about how good things can look. Let's assume that BetaCam is 100 in terms of quality.

If we used a 3-chip DV camera, we might get to 90 or 92, assuming good lighting conditions. If you used a single-chip DV camera, you're looking at 75 to 80, in terms of the quality. The BetaCam, if you were to hire a crew, would probably cost you at least $1,500-$2,000 a day. If you hired somebody with a DV camera, you might end up hiring some kid that bought this system for $3,000 and is willing to work for $100 a day. The costs for camera crews can vary widely. There's also a difference in the quality of the people you use, so make sure that you have competent people that are shooting your product for you.

Here are the 4 main points to creating a video product:

- Always hire professionals
- Have backup equipment
- The script is everything
- Time is expensive.

Don't do what I did the first time. When I started to create my first video, I hadn't finished the script. I was just winging it. It used up a lot of time and I was paying people by the hour. Bad move. Have everything done ahead of time.

Before you decide to produce a video in any form ask yourself if what you're thinking of doing has a strong VISUAL component. Sounds logical, but a lot of people make mistakes in this area. I was shocked to see a video from a supposed expert in the organizational field. This individual produced a video where they spent their entire time looking straight into the camera and talking.

This is ABSURD.

Videos should be produced and used when it makes sense. The topic of organization would be PERFECT for a video. Why not show me a closet or a garage or office space before the organizational guru has shown up. Then show me how it was transformed into a model of organizational excellence. This would make a lot of sense. Unfortunately this individual did not talk to me before starting this project. Bad idea.

Over the last 10+ years I've produced over 200 videos for myself and my clients. This is an area I know a lot about. NEVER try and do it yourself for first few times.

If you do choose to go it alone after that, get some MAC equipment. I suggest a high end desktop system, a big monitor and Imovie software. Purists will tell you to use Final Cut Pro. I disagree. Go with the very simple and easy to use Imovie. It will do everything you need and you can learn how to use it in a couple of hours.

Once you shoot and edit your digital video you'll then have to choose what "form" to put it in. You can either put it in standard video tape form, or you can produce a DVD. Again, Apple has the ideal solution for the novice or non-professional. Use IDVD. It is a simple program that will allow you to prepare professional looking DVD's with a minimum of effort and cost.

Computer Programs

The best part about creating a computer program is the low cost to sales ratio. Once you have the product created, it costs you about $1 to produce and you can sell it for anything from $49 to $199 or even more. That's as much as a 1 to 200 ratio. That's pretty sweet. That's the kind of product we're looking for. You can get people going to the web, downloading your program all day long, and getting paid for work that you did once and never have to do again. It's a beautiful thing.

My friend Armand Morin is the master of this area of information product creation. He finds a need that people has and goes on www.renta-coder.com or www.scriptlance.com . He puts out a bid for a program that he wants created and he gets people bidding on his job.

Recently, he created a piece of software for $150 that he sold $100,0000 worth of it in 60-90 days after he released it. Brilliant.

Look for solutions that people want in your niche market and put out bids on the various sites I've listed above. Get a piece of software created for you that you OWN the rights to and sell a few copies to recover your cost. After that, it's all gravy!

I recently went to a real estate seminar and found a need that people had that wasn't being addressed. All of the gurus who spoke at this event talked about the need to buy properties that had a positive cash flow. None of them sold or told people about a tool to assess a piece of property. So, I went and had a template created. I then took the spreadsheet template and handed it over to someone who created an online program that people can use to plug in their numbers to see if they work.

In order to use the program, they must "sign-up." This way I have their email addresses and can send them offers that relate to real estate investing.

Surprise! The name of the site? www.DoTheNumbersWork.com. I also reserved the site: www.RealEstateInvesmentCalculator.com. They both go to the same place. How much did I pay to have the programmer create this site from the Excel spreadsheet I had put together? $100.

How much money will this site make me? I expect it will generate hundreds of times that amount each year once I generate a large number of opt-in names.

I have also just launched a site called www.MemberScript.com. This is a piece of software designed to help anyone who wants to put together a membership site. It cost a lot of money to develop but I'm 100% certain it will pay for itself in the first 90 days.

I hired programmers to help me put this program together because I knew what I (and my other friends in the information marketing business) wanted and was certain there would be demand for it.

Look for similar opportunities in your niche!

Seminars

A seminar is an experiential product. That means it's a hands-on, has to be experienced in person, product. It's a great way to get people to pay to be prospects. What I mean by this is that people may sign up for your event having never bought anything before from you and then end up buying a number of other things you sell. They not only paid you to come to your event, they ended up buying more "stuff" as well.

Seminars are one of my strong suits and they make great information products. It's one of those products that we sell to people as part of our total product mix. Seminars are a great way to make money and to highlight yourself, your knowledge and your services to potential buyers – buyers who have paid to be there!! It's a great way to make money, on several levels.

You do NOT make your money on having a seminar alone. You have to understand the formula which is TR=SR+PS+CB. Total Revenue is equal to Seminar Registration PLUS Product Sales PLUS Consulting Business. That means that the seminar's profitability is not just determined by what most people think, which is TR=SR (Total Revenue equals Seminar Registration).

If you don't sell any products to people at your events, you are missing a huge revenue opportunity and you're also letting your customers down. If you deliver good information at your seminar, people will want more from you. Allow them to purchase more from you – this is the PS in our formula.

Seminar Registration is how most people paid to come to your event. The product sales side can be high, and in my case I'm really good at selling products, so oftentimes it would behoove me to be doing 200 person events, even for free, in order to get product sales going.

Now the CB portion of the formula is Consulting Business, and that's something that will result over time. If we look at our funnel system, you will see that consulting business is down at the end of our funnel – the expensive end. Occasionally, if you do a seminar somebody will call you up and say "Hey, I want you to do some consulting work for me". But it usually doesn't happen immediately after the event. Many times, it takes a month, two months, 3 years, or even 5 years. So really look at TR=SR+PS and leave the CB as sort of "gravy" money that you get from seminars that are on the back end. They are a component that will kick in eventually. I just don't want you to expect them or compute them in your standard assessment of how profitable a seminar will be. To learn more about consulting, you can buy my book "Consulting Secrets to Triple Your Income" through amazon.

Never withhold information if you're in a seminar environment. You will occasionally see seminar leaders who want to drum up consulting business play this game. Somebody at a table will say,

"Well, Fred, what do you think about blah blah blah?" And you'll say "Well, you know, if you hire me as a consultant I'll be glad to give you all that information." That is an absolute BS way to get consulting business. Please do not play this kind of game. It only hurts you in the long run. Remember my advice about giving 10 times the value for the money? This is one of those times you need to remember that advice.

What you need to do is be as forthcoming as possible. Give answers as completely as you can, because when you do, what will people think? There must be more. So don't hold back information. Never, ever, ever do it. When people pay you to give them information, give it all to them, as much as you can, as richly as possible, because they deserve it.

I frequently use seminars as a front end in a market. Many times, it is the first thing I offer to people in a given market. I did it in catering and I did it in the self-storage industry. Rather than offering them the low end product, the $10 product, I went in and offered them a 1-day seminar at $297. If I were coaching myself, I probably wouldn't do that because my profitability, although good, was limited compared to stimulating people to come to my web site, give me $10 for a report and trading them up sequentially. It probably would have been a much wiser move.

But, you can use seminars as a front end, particularly if you're a really good presenter. You can use seminars and free seminars as a means of getting people in the door and then selling them things or selling them on a future event or selling them on a consulting service or any other product you offer. I frequently will use it as my front end, especially since this is my strongest suit. It's what I do best. I love speaking and am a great speaker, therefore I have a tendency to rely on that as the front end product. If that's your strongest suit also, you may want to do the same, but I don't recommend it as a policy for everyone.

Seminars work best if promoted via an opt-in mailing list. I have moved almost entirely to a model in the seminar business where I only do e-mail marketing as a means of getting people to come to seminars. E-mail marketing is most effective because it's free to do if you have everyone's e-mail addresses. However, if you have been doing this for 15 years like I have you may not have email addresses for a large part of your database.

My challenge now is to convert all those physical mail address customers into e-mail customers. I'm probably going to make some kind of an outrageous offer to the entire list of people without e-mail addresses that says "Look. If you give me your e-mail address, I'm going to give you a hell of a good deal on something. I'm going to give you something for free." I will do this because the value of their email address will be worth more to me than the value of the product I am giving to them.

I have two groups of people. And you will too. You will have prospects and you will have customers. A prospect is somebody who has not bought anything from you. A customer is somebody who's bought anything from you. All I care about getting from a prospect is their e-mail address. For customers, I need to have their full physical address. Let me repeat that. Prospects, the only thing you have to care about is e-mail addresses. Customers, you want to have their entire address. And why is that? Because we don't want to be marketing to prospects through expensive means like direct mail and other things that require postage. We want to instead do it through inexpensive means – like the opt-in mailing list.

You've got to remember one thing in the seminar business. If somebody says they're going to show up for a seminar and they haven't paid, their chances of showing up are less than 100%. If someone pays to attend, their chances of showing up are less than 100%, but are certainly much better if they've paid. You want to encourage people to pay – in any way that is convenient for them.

For more information on how to promote your seminar, get my program on Marketing and Promoting Seminars at www.seminarexpert.com. That's an entire one-day seminar devoted entirely to marketing and promoting seminars. You can also take a look at a much more complete discussion of the topic at: www.seminaronseminars.com. That's a 3 day audio recording of one of my bootcamps on the topics of seminars. My point is, seminars should be one item in your information marketing arsenal. It should be one of the things you sell.

Bootcamps

The term "bootcamp" has been in vogue for the last few years. It is a term that is generally used for a multi-day event that has more than one speaker and that provides in-depth information about a given topic.

They are best promoted by joint e-mail marketing. Let's say you know of a group of 20 information gurus that each had a list of 5,000 customers on their e-mail list. And let's say that all 5,000 of those customers were interested in becoming a self-published author. If I was going to do a self-publishing bootcamp out in Las Vegas, I'd go to each of the gurus and say "Hey, folks, here's the deal. This seminar's going to cost $777. I'm willing to make the following deal with you. If you send this out to your list, I will set you up as an affiliate for this particular seminar, and you'll get 50% of the registration dollars."

Why would I do this? Why would I give 50% of my registration dollars away? Because I got people to show up at my event without any out-of-pocket costs on my part. Remember, the traditional means of marketing seminars involves direct mail, radio, and TV – the kind of advertising where you actually have to pay for it upfront. This way, my marketing becomes a pure variable cost rather than a fixed cost. If I go to each of them and joint venture, I will gladly give them 50% of the registration dollars because 1) I want them to get excited about promoting this event, and 2)it costs me nothing, virtually nothing, to have an additional seats set up in a room if they bring me five people.

PLUS, I still get half the registration fees, which don't include any future consulting business plus any product sales. AND, that customer then becomes mine. So I'm paying them to deliver to me a customer who's ripe and ready to buy my services and products.

The original lists will remain their lists. They will not have access to my names and I will not have access to theirs. They will send a message to their entire database of 5,000 people with a link embedded in the text that says "Hey. There's this great event coming here. If you want to know more about it, click here." When someone clicks there from their e-mail list onto my machine, my machine knows which guru it is coming from and, if they sign up, that guru gets a piece. The only names on these lists that I will ever have access to are the ones who signed up for my seminar. And at that point they become my client as well.

A note of caution: be very careful when you work with other speakers. If you haven't heard them speak before, take a pass. Even if you have heard them speak, some speakers are good at their delivery but are pains in the ass to work with. This isn't fun. I don't work with these types of people anymore.

Do I pay my speakers? No. Speakers come for free. Why? They have funnels and they have products to sell at these events. Guess what? If you show up at my event, and you have a product to sell, we are splitting the revenue from those product sales 50-50. For example, if you have a product for $300 and you sell 30 sets of those and make nine grand, you and I are splitting that revenue 50-50. So I get $4,500 and you get $4,500.

Remember, revenue as a seminar promoter comes to me from several different areas:

1. Seminar registration via joint e-mail marketing and my own list.
2. Product sales via speakers at the event. It's a straight 50-50 split.
3. Consulting business that might come to me and be generated by me as a result of having participants attend the seminar.

How do you get speakers to show up? You won't get some speakers because they don't get it. They don't understand that you have a product to sell. If they don't have products to sell, they're not going to be a speaker at my event!

Every once in a while, I may have a real high profile individual that wants to speak at my event and they're willing to speak for free and not sell products. OK. That's fine. But you know what? That kind of speaker isn't making us any money as a group, or making himself or herself any money, or making me any money as an individual. Take a close look at a speaker like that before you allow them to join your panel.

Certifications/Designations

People love to have designations after their names: MBA, PhD, CPA, etc. About the only certification I think is worthwhile is that of an MD, and sometimes I'm not even sure about that one. From the standpoint of getting certifications yourself, I think that most of them are a massive waste of time.

In the speaking industry, where I spend a lot of my time there are two designations or certifications that they give speakers. One is a C.S.P. The certified speaking professional. You have to submit a mountain of paperwork, kiss enough behinds, and you can put these letters after your name. Is there any verifiable measurement that will show you that this helps to get you booked as a speaker? None that I'm aware of. There is still another designation in the speaking business called a C.P.A.E. This stands for "Certified Peer Award of Excellence." Again, the same thing. Nothing can be proven that these folks make more money or get more speaking engagements.

In some industries, certifications may mean something to one's peers, but RARELY to one's clients. I've never seen anyone ask my accountant for his C.P.A. Good thing. He doesn't have one! Does that prevent him from being an excellent accountant or financial advisor? Not at all.

But, the fact remains that people LIKE to get these certifications and designations. If that's the case, why not create one and sell it to them? If you do create one, make sure that it means something to both clients and peers or it will be tough to sell.

For plastic surgeons, consumers actually seem to care (from my experience) if someone is "Board Certified" or not. If you create designations, make them challenging enough to have them mean something. Even if they are tough for people to attain and actually have value, it will take a while to get clients to see there value even if there is any value at all.

The best way to create and sell certifications and designations is to set up an association. There's no mystery to setting up your own association. Pick out a name, make sure it's available (both on and off line) and then set up a bank account in that associations name. By having the association, you can appoint/anoint yourself the President of that association.

And remember: certification will not protect your clients from liability. In fact, it probably makes your liability even greater. Why? If you are certified you are supposed to be an expert in that field and above making mistakes! It's something you must consider carefully.

But if you offer certification, it can be a HUGE money maker. There is no limit to what you can charge people. It all depends on the industry you're in and what the market will bear. I've seen certification programs go for a low of $195 to a high of well over $1,000. The more you charge, the more "stuff" you'll have to give people for attaining that status. On the low end you'll need to give them a fancy piece of paper with their name on it. On the high end you may need to go out and have a fancy, relatively expensive plaque designed and produced.

Many years ago I was asked to help write the qualifications questions for people who were looking to get certified in the clinical nutrition field. I was not involved in writing anything but the marketing questions for this group. God knows, that was all I was qualified to do.

The written test was part of what people needed to gain a specific designation form this organization in the nutrition field.

If you're interested in starting your own association and doing certification, you may want to check out: www.startyourownassociation.com. I've put together an audio program that will help you immensely in this area.

Speaking Engagements

The funnel system has speaking engagements and consulting business at the bottom of the funnel. It may be the bottom in terms of it's position, but it is the most lucrative. the two big, big money items. Speaking engagements and high end consulting are the places where you make the big money. Let' talk about speaking here. In this section I'm talking about the more traditional speaking engagements that you might get as opposed to your own self promoted seminars.

There are four items that you need to have as a speaker:
- A demo video
- A profile sheet
- A press kit
- A website

The first is a demo video. This is a video that shows people how good you are at doing what you do. The demo video should run anywhere from eight to twelve minutes. It should have snippets and recordings of one or more events that you've packaged in a very clever and creative fashion to highlight your abilities and your overall expertise in your subject matter.

You cannot set up a video recorder and record your demo in your basement because it's going to look cheap and amateurish. I occasionally put together a group of people who want to "co-op" a video production session. You may want to set up something similar with a group of people you know. What I'm suggesting is getting 10 or 12 people together, and pool our funds to hire a crew. Each of us will pay $1,000 and get twenty or thirty minutes in front of the group.

You're going to "stage" the whole thing. Each member of the group needs to be ready with their best thirty minutes of material. Each member brings at least ten friends for their audience, and they have to sit through the whole thing. They can't leave when you're done. Because people who speak at 8:30 in the morning deserve the same size audience as people who speak at 4:30 in the afternoon. We may have two different sets. We may change the position to make it look like we're in two different places. You'll bring two changes of clothes. And what it allows you to do is have a demo video created inexpensively. I'm going to start doing it about once a year. That way, we can all get professionally-produced demo videos for a fraction of the cost.

The second thing you need is something called a "one sheet" or a "profile sheet". It's a single page, front and back, which gives people the following information:

- Your name
- Your picture
- Background or bio
- Your topics, and a blurb on each one with a few bullet points (Don't do more than four topics on this sheet because it makes you look like a "Jack of all Trades, Master of None")
- A list of your clients
- Some testimonials
- Elements of why you are unique and different

Generally, the profile sheet should be written in the third person. You can produce them in color but you should certainly have a black and white version. Why? Because some people may want them to have them faxed to them, and most people don't have color faxes. You'll also want to have them available in digitally deliverable PDF format.

The third thing you need is a press kit. A press kit is like a presentation folder - it's got all your stuff in it. What goes in a press kit?

- Articles you've written
- Articles written about you
- Testimonial letters
- Copy of a book
- Anything and Everything that makes you look good

Finally, you need to have a web site with all of your info. Why? Because people expect it in this day and age, you can have up-to-the-minute information added to it easily, people can download your products like e-Books, and because it cuts down the cost of mailing to people. You'll also want potential clients to be able to download or view (in a streaming fashion), your video.

You have two ways of promoting yourself as a speaker: Direct and Indirect.

Direct business will come as a result of you trading people up your funnel in terms of the price points. It is a natural result that someone will hire you for a speaking engagement if they bought some of your other material or attended a workshop, or otherwise traded themselves up the ladder.

Let's say I bought your report for $10. The report was pretty damned good. I was impressed, so I bought your book for $25. And I said "Boy, this is really good stuff, too." And let's say you had a monthly newsletter and I signed up for that. After that, I came to one of your seminars and bought a video and I bought some other products and material. And I own a company that's got 2,000 employees. After doing all that, I say "You know, I want to have you come in and talk to all of my employees directly about a topic. We're going to have you in for three days and we're going to pay you five grand a day." Not unusual to have this happen if you've got this whole thing set up. Is it difficult? No, it just requires a little time and effort.

Speaking engagements are a high-end service that will result from you selling niche market information products. Here's another example. Earlier in the day a guy who had gotten my name from a friend called me. He wanted to see if I would be available to speak to a group of real estate speakers on the topic of Selling Products from the Platform. How did I even get consideration for this "gig"? I have a book out on the topic. As a result of the book, one of his friends had bought one of my other audio programs and when the subject came up, he recommended me to his friend. He wants me to speak to his group for one day at some 3-day event that he's having. My rate for this engagement will be a minimum guarantee of $7,000 for the day. This is a textbook example of how these things can work.

The other way to get speaking engagements is through a Speaking Bureau. Bureaus are non-exclusive agents for speakers and, in general, their fees range anywhere from 20 to 30%. It's absolute highway robbery. They are getting away with 20 to 30% of your fees. For instance, if I get booked at five grand, I only make $3,500 plus my expenses.

All the bureau does is to look for clients. So a client will call in and say "Hey I need a couple speakers on this topic and this topic and this topic." What happens then? The speaker's bureau people say, "Oh, you need customer service speakers? Let me send you these twenty tapes." They throw as much as they can up against the wall hoping it will stick, because they don't really care. They're indiscriminate. A good speaker's bureau will try to be very discerning about figuring out exactly what the client wants and who's the right mix with the right speaker. But many of them won't do work that hard.

By the way, most bureaus, in my humble opinion, are dramatically overpaid for the work they do. In the future I would like to arrange it so I never have to deal with a speaker's bureau. Some of them are pretty good. But most of them charge outrageous fees for minimal effort. And, of course, saying that gets me in trouble every time I voice it. But I don't care because I don't want to give you anything less than the truth.

Take a look at the sites: www.professionalspeakingsuccess.com or www.speakingformillions.com for more information and help in this area.

You can also speak at other people's events who give seminars. I'm a regular on the "circuit". People invite me to speak, I pay my own way their and then get 50% of the gross sales I do. To be asked to speak at other people's events you must be both good at selling from the platform and deliver a lot of good content.

Tele-Seminars

Teleseminars are seminars that are conducted over the phone. They are simple and easy to do. Before you get started, you have some basic choices to make first. Do you do them for free or charge people? Do you use a free service or pay for a dedicated "teleseminar" phone line? How long should they be? All of these good questions and deserve to be answered.

Regardless of your answers to those questions, you'll want to record any teleseminar you do for possible future sale.

How long should a teleseminar be? It depends on how much you're charging people. Should it be multi day? Again, this will depend on how much you charged and how much perception of value you're trying to create.. I would never go longer than 90 minutes on the phone at one time. I have done teleseminars that went on for 4 hours, but we had two breaks during the session.

Free or paid teleseminar line?

Free or Paid

You have two choices when you do a teleseminar. Free or fee. If you do a teleseminar for free you've got to have something to sell them on the back-end to have it make sense economically.

When Free? When Paid?

Want to learn more about teleseminars? Get in touch with my friend and client, Preston Campbell. He's put together the definitive course on the topic. His website is www.Teleseminar.com.

Tele-seminars are a great way to get paid for your time without leaving your home. Additionally, the attendees don't have to spend time or money on travel. What exactly is a tele-seminar? It is the ability to have many people calling into the same line and taking part in a seminar, discussion group, group coaching, or whatever. Do whatever the heck you want with it – there's almost no limit to the formats you can use.

I use and recommend that you try a service called: www.freeconference.com. The service is free. There is also a service called www.freeconferencecall.com. You'll also want to

You can get up to 100 people can be on this line simultaneously. They call in with passwords, and all get access to the seminar, or discussion group or whatever. That line is yours to use 24 hours a day, 7 days a week, 365 days a year.

You can also contract with different places to lease your own bridge line. Depending on your needs and usage, this may be a good thing. If you do lease your own line, you can charge others to use it. I know one person who's got six people using his line. The guy told me that in one year he made $2,500 off of his tele-seminars line. I said, "God bless you." He bought a line and then he sold the line by days of the week saying "OK, you're Monday, you're Tuesday, you're Wednesday, you're Thursday, you're Friday, you're Saturday, and you're Sunday. Give me 500 bucks each. You have it for the year." So that's what he's doing. Pretty interesting, huh?

With tele-seminars, you can do multiple coaching events, you can do free events, and you can do things at the last minute. You send out an e-mail and say, "The first 30 people to call in will talk about "X".

We're going to do it for an hour, 4-5 Eastern Time." Boom. Just get people. It's really a cool thing to be able to do. You can do them free, you can charge for them, or you make people pay in advance. You know, I've seen tele-seminars where people are paying 97 bucks for a 90-minute tele-seminar. Maybe $350 for a series of eight weeks that goes every Wednesday night. Use your imagination. It's a great thing to do.

A coaching client of mine, Preston Campbell, has a very good program on this topic. Take a look at www.teleseminarsuccess.com. It's a great course on the topic if you want more in this area.

One-on-One Coaching

I used to use a very traditional coaching model. I'd give people my monthly fee and they would then talk to me every week or 10 days for that flat fee. As a general rule I would meet with them 3 or 4 times a month and get my flat monthly fee. That was then, this is now.

I now offer only ONE kind of coaching. It's my lifetime coaching arrangement. I only offer this one level of coaching because I want to deal only with SERIOUS clients. People who are willing to work and where there is a good match between us. For more information on how this program works, take a look at www.TheProductGuru.com.

In my coaching program, people give me $5,000 up front and then pay me $15,000 as they make the money from our efforts together. Let's say someone signs up today. They give me a non-refundable $5k. Then next month as a result of our efforts they generate $1,000. They send me a check for $500. The following month they generate $2,000. They send me a check for $1,000. And so on until they "pay off" the $5,0000 in deferred payments.

After they generate $40,000 as a result of our efforts, they then give me 5% per month. This is only after I've made them twice what they've paid me.

Very few people do a coaching program as I described above. I am one of few who can pull this off because I'm a well known entity in my field. It would be a wise idea to START with a monthly coaching arrangement. Start by charging people somewhere around $500 a month and give them unlimited access. Unlimited access? Am I crazy by suggesting you do this? Hardly

I learned this from a good friend of mine who's a very, very famous and well-known coach. And he said to me "Fred, here's what happens. When you give people unlimited ability to call and e-mail you, the total number of hours you spend on the phone with clients will go down and the perception of value will go up." You as a client feel that you have the right to call me at any time or e-mail me and ask me questions. But I also have the right, as a coach, to say, "Hey, I'm busy. Can I get back to you? Let's set up a time, blah, blah, blah."

I know people that have minimum coaching fees of $2,000 a month. You go to Tony Robbins and it's a million dollars a year. He's got fourteen or fifteen people in that program. A million dollars each, OK? It's all a matter the benefit your clients feel their getting from your services.

In my coaching contract it specifically states that this isn't therapy or counseling or anything like that. It's specifically setting up objectives for people to reach business goals, and helping them arrive at those objectives. I'm not serving in a therapist or a clergy capacity. That's not my role. In fact, when I talk to my clients, I give them assignments to complete. If they call me before they've completed their assigned task I will politely remind them that they must do THEIR part before they call me back. I suggest you do the same with your clients.

I also provide them with access to the my resources. Basically, I'm opening up my Rolodex to them and saying "Here's who you need to call and who you need to go to." I'm giving them my time and my energy and my expertise over the phone in exchange for my coaching fees and percentage. If anyone needs to purchase certain products or services, it's going to cost them additional dollars.

Do some people need credentials to coach? Probably. Do YOU need these credentials to coach? Probably not. I have never taken any coaching courses.

You must have your client sign a written coaching contract and usually get the first three months payment in advance. Before I changed my model I went to a four month advance retainer. Four months up front, non-cancelable. Non-refundable. The contract is cancelable only after the first four months. But you must deliver value, and your clients have made a two grand commitment.

Most of the people who find me for coaching usually have come to one of my seminars, seen me at one of my events, read some of my material, or have listened to some of my audio programs. I do not go out and actively solicit coaching business. I think it's the wrong way to market it, although some people would disagree. Some people will offer on their web site a free coaching session. You get on the phone and that works very well for some people. My coach does that.

Now, you may be wondering how I can be a coach and still need a coach. Or for that matter, what a coach can do for me. Well, as for being a coach, I have plenty of expertise and contacts and a lot of value to impart to others. That does not mean that I don't need my own coach, however.

I tend to get scattered – have ideas running all over the place. My coach helps to keep me centered and focused. I have a client that I was yelling at on the phone the other day. She came back from this event and she was full of ideas – all beyond her current abilities. And I said, "Look! Cut it out! I want to stop talking about all this future crap and concentrate on what needs to get done now. I don't want to talk about anything in the future until we get done with business right now. Enough of this futurizing. We're not going to be able to look at the future until we get the present done now." And, so that's the same thing that my coach does for me. He makes me concentrate on specific tasks that I need to take care of now.

He also gives me accountability so that at the end of a week or two I call and the first question is "What have you done on x, y or z since last we spoke? What did you do? How's it gotten done? What obstacles did you encounter? What help did you need?"

I've got a site that I'm opening up that's called www.coachingasabusiness.com.   I will interview 16 of the top coaches in the country as relates to how they market their services. And what's in it for them? They get to give out their contact information.

Let's say I record 16 people and they each give me an hour of audio. That's 16 hours of my time. I'm going to sell that program all day long for $397, no sweat. The top 16 coaches spill their guts for an hour each. Man, I can write a hell of a sales letter for this. This is going to be a no-brainer to get people who are interested in coaching. Those people that are disappointed in their coaches weren't given value. This is going to be value!!

So here's my method for finding the top coaches. I will do a search on the Internet, which is how you should do it as well. I will go to google.com and I will put in "business coaching" or "business coaches" and I will see who comes up in the top 100. I will contact them. I will give them the deal, which is they get no money. It's an interview; they can give out their contact information. If they don't get it, click. Move to the next. Whoever agrees to the deal, they're going to get interviewed.

So, I'm asking you to do the same thing with your clients. Think about how you can create real, true, authentic value in what you do. And if you do that, people will come back to you again, and again, and again and buy more, and more, and more stuff.

Consulting

Let me first differentiate between my definition of consulting and coaching. Coaching is helping someone in a one-on-one situation. Consulting is where you work with an organization or an association as opposed to an individual.

The best way to get consulting business is to have people come to you. The same thing is true in the consulting field. The worst way to get consulting (or coaching) work is to go out begging for it. Do it that way and you'll look needy. And when you look needy, I don't care if it's in a personal relationship or in business, it's a bad thing. People will not want to hang out with you, not want to do business with you, not want to be around you if you look like a sponge bucket of need. It just won't work.

I'll give you a perfect example of how I keep from looking needy. I recently responded to an e-mail from a guy in the self storage industry. He happens to be based in Puerto Rico and has 3 facilities down there. I said, "By the way, you ought to have me come down there and do some training for your staff" because I'm thinking to myself that it was getting cold and I wouldn't mind a trip to Caribbean.

Not long thereafter e calls me up and he says, "You know, I'm considering maybe having you come in. What would you charge me for that?" And I said, "Well, I don't know. Puerto Rico, if I get to come in the winter, you might be able to get me for five grand for a couple of days if you pay all the expenses." And he said "Oh really? Why should I use you?" And I said, "Because I'm the best." He says "Well aren't you going to say any more about that?" I said "No. I don't need your business; I don't need your money. If you don't want to hire me, hire someone else." I said, "Frankly, I have low fixed overhead, I have a place in Las Vegas, I have a place in New York. I'm very comfortable. If you give me no money whatsoever, I'm not going to die. I don't need your money. Next question?"

That's what I said to him over the phone. This has done one of two things. Either he thinks I'm an obnoxious arrogant jerk, which he probably does anyway, or he might think "You know what – this guy probably is good enough that he doesn't care".

The point to all of this is that I DO have low overhead and that I don't need his money. If you keep your overhead low, it gives you the ability to tell people to go take a flying leap.

Also, it's a hell of a marketing tool! To be able to say to people "You know what? The heck with you! I don't need you! Go take a hike!" You know what? Those same people that you say that to will come back begging for you later.

For example, I talked to a woman recently on the phone. She was a referral from a lawyer friend of mine. She's got a whole line of video and audio products she wants to produce and my friend the lawyer asked me at this event how much I would charge her for a complete marketing plan. I said, "I don't know. Maybe twenty five grand." She said "Wow. That's a lot of money." I said "Well, that's what I charge."

So this woman calls me but had not been given my price; therefore, she wasn't pre-qualified, although I assumed that she was. She was one of those overly-organized, detail-oriented people with a million questions, and kept me on the phone for nearly an hour without really getting down to business. After I told her the fee and she gasped, and I said, "Oh, Susan didn't tell you what the fees were?" She said "No. I had no idea". I said, "Well, yes, you can probably get it done cheaper, but you can't get it done better." I said, "You know. That's what it will cost you." And she said, "Well, how much to actually implement some of the marketing plan?" I said "If you put 50 or 60 thousand dollars aside, 25 for my fee and the rest for the actual testing and implementation, that would probably be a good amount."

After talking to this woman on the phone and later getting an e-mail from her, I seriously doubt that even if she gives me the $50,000.00 that I'm going to work with her. I'd love to have the money and I know I can use it for a lot of fun stuff and give it away to a lot of great causes, but this woman is a royal pain as I perceive her. She may not be, but I perceive her as being very, very difficult to work with. And you know what? My overhead is low enough that I want to be able to say "Sorry. I'm just not the right guy."

And what will happen when I do that? She's going to come back begging. The moral of this story is that you should probably have a "pain in the ass fee" in your rate structure; for anyone who's a pain in the ass to work with, you should charge double your usual rate. If they're willing to pay it, I guess you just suck it up. You deal with them. I'm completely serious here.

What I should have said to her was something like this: "You're probably looking at fifty grand." Because basically what I wanted to say is "You know what? I don't really want to work with you, but if you're willing to give me $50,000.00, I think I can suck it up." I'll take twenty five thousand up front, twenty five thousand upon delivery and I will put a contract together than will state for this woman exactly how many hours of each month she can talk to me over the phone or take up my time with e-mail messages. This woman would be on the phone with me two hours a day, unless I said otherwise. I would say, "I'm going to have to send you a contract with the specifics of the arrangement and I want you to go over it carefully."

When are you consulting and when are you just giving free friendly advice? If they ask for it, they pay for it. If they ask for the first meeting, it's on them. If somebody called me out of the blue tomorrow and said "Fred, I need some of your time to discuss a matter, this could turn into a big project for you." I'd say "Oh that's great. I'd be more than happy to meet you. My hourly rate for an initial consultation is $295 for the hour." They say "Oh, well, this is the beginning." I'd say "That's fine. If we actually end up working together and the fee is more than three or four thousand dollars, I refund you the initial fee. No problem. Now do you want to send me a copy of the agenda? When would you like to meet?" If they balk at that, you don't have a real prospect. You've got somebody who's trying to pick your brain.

I always use this story and I love telling it, so you'll have to indulge me. Here's what consulting is like. Consulting is like selling. Imagine if you walked into Tom McCann and say for the last twenty years you've been buying shoes from Tom McCann. You walk into Tom McCann tomorrow and you pick out two pairs of shoes and you walk up to the counter and you say to the cashier "You know. I've been buying shoes here at Tom McCann for the last twenty years. Today, I think I deserve these two pairs of shoes for free." Now, if you're here in New York City, do you know what they're going to say to you? "Right over here. You're not going to get those shoes for free anywhere."

But do you know what? That's what people try to do to you as a consultant. I'd like you to picture that in your brain there are tiny little racks filled with tiny little shoes. And here's what people will try to do to you either over the phone or in person. They try and shake you and get those tiny little shoes that are in your head to fall off those tiny little shelves and fall out of your ears. And they're sitting there with their hands ready to catch your tiny little shoes. And those shoes are your inventory. The only thing you have to sell as a consultant is your knowledge, your brainpower, and your expertise that you have accumulated over the past years. When people ask for free advice, they are trying to steal your inventory - your tiny little shoes. And what you need to do is tell people that you don't give away shoes for free.

I want you to remember that analogy. When somebody's trying to shake you for information, what they're trying to do is steal your inventory. They're trying to steal your tiny little shoes. And usually when I tell that story no one ever forgets. Somebody came up to me after thirteen years and remembered the tiny little shoe story!

Now, that doesn't mean that on occasion you won't give away a pair of free shoes if you think there's a lot of other shoes that you can sell. But you should make that determination - don't let people shake your shoe tree without you knowing it. Don't let anyone steal your inventory. If you want to give it away that's your choice. But don't let people steal it from you.

On the other hand, if I ask for the first meeting, then I pay for it. In other words, if I approach American Express and say, "Hey, I got some great ideas", then the first meeting is on me.

The best sales method is word of mouth – having the names and phone numbers of satisfied customers as well as testimonial letters. That will sell it for you better than any promotional material you have. Consulting is the natural result of trading people up to higher and higher price products in this system. Look at your funnel system. Consulting is at the bottom. When people buy all the other stuff, consulting is the natural next step. That's how it should go.

I'll give you an example. I have someone who entered my funnel by buying one of my books in the self-storage industry for $99 from Amazon. He came to one of my seminars and after coming to one of my seminars, he hired me to come over to Australia to do consulting work for him for $4,500.00 a day plus expenses. That's a sweet deal, but it generally takes a few more bumps up the ladder before it goes there. Usually, somebody doesn't buy a $99 (or any other low end product) book and then call you for a $5,000 day consultation, but it can happen!

Before you try and generate consulting business you'll need some basic tools. The most basic of your promotional tools is your book. A book is an instant credibility builder as well as the best "business card" you can possibly have. You've got to have one.

When people ask you whether or not you consult, if you want to say yes, you'll have to be prepared when they ask you to send them something. You should have some standard methods of response. A standard fax, a standard e-mail, a standard contract, all ready to go so that if somebody asks for these things, you can immediately get it to them and get them to sign on the dotted line.

I have a complete program on how to start and build a web-based consulting business at www.consultingexpert.com.

Selling Other People's Products

If you want to get into the information products business and don't have anything to sell, you can always sell other peoples products. Even after you start producing your own products, you may like a certain product so much that you continue to sell it.

To sell other peoples products you can either become an affiliate for that person or you can license the product for you to sell. If you set yourself up as an affiliate, you'll send people to that individual's website with your tracking code attached. If and when someone buys, you'll automatically get credit.

If you don't have your own products to sell, what should you do? Sit on your duff and do nothing? Absolutely NOT. Become an affiliate for someone else's products. Perhaps event buy a license from someone. Let's say that I bought a mortgage calculation product. What would I want next? As the information marketer selling the product, I had better know what the next product is and get a hold of it so that when somebody calls me on the phone and places a $49 or a $99 order, I can say "By the way, would you like this product today?" Or if I have a database of customers who buy the product I can say to them "By the way, blah, blah, blah ... we can now sell you this." You want to have a stream of products starting at the low-end going to the high-end, and all points in between.

So, as the marketer of this particular information product, what would I have in my arsenal? I would have a joint venture with a mortgage broker and get a finders fee of $500 for anybody who closes on a mortgage. I would also look at real estate agents, etc. I would want to make sure that my sales and revenue potential were maximized.

There you have it. Those are virtually all the information products you can create. Now let's learn how to market and sell them!

Marketing and Selling Your Info Products

Introduction

Now that you've learned how to determine your niche and create your information products, the next logical step is to figure out how to SELL them.

Let's talk about the actual sales process. You must offer products at different price points and using different modalities. But you must have a system to fill your funnel and then trade people up automatically. Your initial effort should be to get people into your funnel. After you get them in the funnel, you'll need a separate system for trading people up the product ladder.

To fill your funnel, start with those methods that are the least expensive. You want to start with the least expensive methods to fill your funnel and those that fit your personality the best. For example, if you really like writing, then you may want to concentrate on article writing as one of your means to fill the funnel. I just wrote an article for a self-storage magazine. I write a marketing article every month. That magazine goes out to about 17,000 people and the only thing I get in exchange for it is a byline, which says, "Fred Gleeck is a profit-maximization consultant in the storage industry. You can get his free tips by going to www.self-storagesuccess.com." Basically, the only thing I want to have happen from that publication is to get people to contact me to put their name into my e-mail system. I also offer them the option of buying my book on self storage marketing.

You may want to look for others to sell your product. The real money in the information marketing business is made in finding what are called affiliates. We used to call them dealers - other people who sell your stuff for you. That's where the real money is made. More about that concept, later.

Before you start filling your funnel you've got to get some of the other basics down. They are listed in order of when you should do them. Have everything set up in advance so that when you start driving people to your site and putting them into your funnel you don't WASTE traffic. Nothing is worse than sending qualified leads to your site before it has been properly set up to maximize your probability of success.

Before Your Start: You Need Systems

You need a system to SELL the information products you've created. You need to put Web Marketing Magic (www.webmarketing-magic.com) into place.

Web Marketing Magic is my program. I licensed it. Someone else wrote the program, but I private-labeled it. In other words, I have my own version of it. But all future enhancements go into the program as well.

I went out looking for a program that could do all the things I needed and I couldn't find it all in one place. When I found it in multiple places, it cost close to $3,300. Web Marketing Magic runs approximately $600 a year, and the other programs, if purchased separately, would have cost me $3,300 a year. Web Marketing Magic was literally a fifth of the cost.

In order to take orders online, you need to spend another $200 for the merchant account. So it's $600 a year with a $200 one-time fee. Then after you pay the $200 there are some monthly fees associated with the credit card merchant system, but that's true wherever you go.

You'll also have to pay your monthly fees to your credit card merchant account plus a small transaction fee per purchase as well as. Plus your percentage, which is 2.97 or something like that. With my merchant account, I not only have to pay a monthly fee, I've got to pay a thirty-cent per transaction fee or 2.97%. So on every $14.95 book that you sell, you make $14.95 minus your cost of all those fees.

What the difference is between this program and a lot of other programs is that it is "server-based". Check my Million Dollar Rolodex under Web Site Design and Web Hosting for my current referral for this service. It is absolutely critical that you get a reliable and creative Web Site designer.

When you start marketing your information products, you must have this as the backbone of your system. Now, let me describe for you a few of the things that this program can do.

Auto Responder

Web Marketing Magic will allow you to get people who sign up something that you offer to receive a series of email messages. To see how this works, send an email to tips@seminarexpert.com. If you do this, I now have your e-mail address. The system will now automatically start sending you a series of emails. As frequently as once a day for as LONG AS YOU WANT.

I have set up autoresponders for every different product I offer. You can and should do the same. Using Web Marketing Magic you can capture as much or as little information as as you like from a client. It's your choice when they sign up to make certain fields required and others optional. The more you ask people to do, the greater the chance you'll irritate them and lose them.

I will send the first message to a client, one day later send another, two days later send another, three days later, eight days later, eighteen days later, 180 days later, 360 days later. There are unlimited numbers of messages that you can load in. So, once you create this process, it's done. Except if you want to tweak it.

How does this fit into the funnel system? Let's say someone buys a report. You have a series of messages set up to send people messages because you want two things to happen. You want to continue to deliver them great content so they respect you and like your material, but every third or fourth message you're going to hit them up with some sort of a little sales pitch.

Why do you have 3 or 4 content messages for every one sales message in your auto responder series? How many of you get e-mail from people that you delete without reading? Why do you delete without reading? Because you feel it's a sales message. If I delivered you three or four content message for every one sales message, are you going to delete my e-mails if you like my stuff? No, because something might be important. You might miss something. You don't want to be deleting what you think is a sales message when it is actually full of content. Let's be clever about this. We want to make sure that we're delivering high quality content so we can sneak in the sales message every so often.

Let's take an example of how an auto responder system works. You buy a report for ten bucks; you bought it today. Immediately the report gets sent to you and two days from now you get something that says "Hey, thanks for buying the report. I thought you might find this important." Two or three more messages with just content and then I say "Oh, by the way. You know what? Since you bought the report you may want to really look at this product." And, I have a link that goes to a web page that has a sales letter that sells the product.

So every third or fourth message you do sales. It's a three or four to one ratio on sales message. Web Marketing Magic will automatically do that and when you buy the book after you bought the report, it will unsubscribe you to that auto responder series and automatically subscribe you to the new one for the book. This new series also gives you good content, three or four to one and then trades up to the next product. Once you buy that, it unsubscribes you from the book and subscribes you to the next products series of letters. Once set up, the system operates automatically. That's why you can go to sleep at night and wake up in the morning with orders in your mailbox.

That's just one feature. That's one feature of a product that costs a total of $600. That one feature alone pays for the system almost immediately. But there's more.

Digital Delivery Module

It will also deliver your digitally delivered products, your PDF stuff, automatically for you through a digital delivery module.

Shopping Cart

The program also has a shopping cart built-in. Since it is server-based, it means that this program doesn't sit on your machine. It sits on a machine out in the sky - a hard disk in cyberspace somewhere. When a customer clicks on something to order, without the customer knowing what's happening, that link goes to this server that sets up what looks like an order page. Now it's not really happening on your computer, but the customer doesn't know. The customer fills out all the information, puts in the credit card information, hits submit and boom. They get the stuff and you're off to the races.

It is like a valet parking situation. You go down to the hotel lobby and say "Here, Ed. Grab my car." The valet parking guy goes and gets your car and delivers it to you immediately. As far as the customer knows, the valet parking service on your web site is instantaneous. They want to order your product, they click on it, the valet guy runs out to the server, brings it back and gives it to the customer. It takes almost no time – it's done in a flash.

Visa/MasterCard Module

You can take Visa and MasterCard with this system. When it comes to credit card orders offline, can you use your merchant account with Marketing Magic? The answer is yes you can. Am I doing it that way? No, I'm not and here's why: I like to maintain two merchant accounts: one online merchant account, and one offline. It's sort of like why your mom told you to bring your umbrella. You never know what's going to happen. So if one of your merchant accounts goes down for whatever reason, you always have a backup.

When I was first getting started I had a merchant account that freaked out when I did a trade show and put over $50k through over a weekend. They shut down my account and wouldn't release the funds. What a nightmare! Trust me; things like this can and DO happen. Expect them. Prepare for them. You always want to have alternative means of getting cash, and that's very, very important.

Client Management System

This system also has a client management system, which has all of your names, e-mail addresses and all the other information on your customers that you have collected. It has a database as well. That's very important for targeting specific groups or clients for marketing messages.

Broadcast Module

The broadcast module allows me to send out an e-mail message to anyone at anytime in any of my groups. That broadcast module allows me to go into any or all of my customer databases and say "I want to send this blanket message to everyone." So, you can have, and I do have, all my different market niches working under one Web Marketing Magic program. The difference between this system and a lot of systems is that if you have more than one niche, you would have to get separate merchant accounts, separate everything. This Web Marketing Magic can handle as many niches as you want, so it's easy to integrate each new market.

Forms

It allows you to set up forms for gathering all the information you want to collect. The forms are already created and easy to adapt to your own needs and situation.

Ad Tracker

A very interesting portion of this module is called an "ad tracker". This is a system that will measure the number of clicks that you get on your product line. Most systems track only traffic hits: the number of people that look at your products.

To collect your free gift, worth $97, send an email to tips@SellingInfoProducts.com

The Web Marketing Magic system tracks not only the number of hits, but also the number of people who order from a given promotion. So, if you get a million clicks and nobody orders, all it does is cause a lot of traffic on your site. But if you get a hundred clicks and 35 orders, that's significant. So this system tracks the number of orders that you receive. It will also do that with an affiliate.

How does it track which affiliate is doing the marketing? You set up different ad trackers. Let's say we have several people who are affiliates. I put an ad tracker on each of their web sites and I would know not only how many hits came from their site, but how many people bought from their site. So it would tell me exactly how many people bought, how many people came from one site versus another site, and who was a more effective affiliate.

Affiliate Module

The affiliate module allows you to set up people as dealers, or affiliates as they call them in the Internet business, to sell your products. All of you want to sell my products? Very simple. You go to Web Marketing Magic and you sign up as an affiliate for Web Marketing. You can only sign up as an affiliate for one particular product. That's the only limitation with this system: if you wanted to sell all of my products, you couldn't. Well, you could, but it's not tracking them.

The affiliate module is put on your site, which links them to my site, where they can buy the product. I know, by the ad tracking module, that you sent the customer to me. My affiliates get 50% of sales generated by them, so if you sold a $100 product, I would know to send you $50.

If you have people who are coming to your site, it's one of the easiest ways to make money there is: All you have to do is refer people to the affiliate site.

Coupon Module

A coupon module allows you to say, "There are only 43 of this item available. Once it's done it's finished." Or to say, "This sale is only going on for the next 72 hours." It's either time or a unit number specific ordering amount after which time it cuts it off and says "Sorry. No more available."

So when you're making a "limited time offer" it isn't just BS. It really is a limited time offer and people will get a message saying "Sorry. All out of that particular item or product." That's a cool feature.

Tell a Friend

It's got a feature that allows you to get people to refer people to you. It's a "tell a friend module". Again, very instrumental in marketing your material on the web.

Unsubscribe

It will unsubscribe people automatically; you don't have to worry about that and do it manually, once the customer requests it. This is extremely important given the new SPAM laws.

Ordering Web Marketing Magic

There is a lot of stuff going on in this Web Marketing Magic system. You cannot order Web Marketing Magic without signing up for a $3.95 thirty-day trial. If you decide you're going to learn how to use it, right after that time, you get access to all the features. But don't check it out until you have thirty days to really devote some time to it or unless you're ready.

Ready means that you have products, you have web sites and that you are in a position to start selling tomorrow.

You only need a skeletal group of products to get started, and I mean no more than 3 or 4, then you can start filling them in and filling them in at different price points. You don't have to wait until you have a complete product line to start.

Other Needed Systems

- You need a system for fulfilling orders offline as well, because you're still going to have to be physically delivering audio and videotape training material.
- You need a system for tracking people – this is your database
- You need a system for tracking money – I use M.Y.O.B. (Mind Your Own Business)
- You need a system for tracking the effectiveness of your advertising and promotional methods. If you're doing it online you can use the ad tracker within WebMarketingMagic. If you're not, you've still got to record where people are coming from.

Your Database

In order to make the most money you possibly can, you'll need to understand your single biggest asset as an information marketer. It's your database! Your list is THE MOST important asset you have. Your database is a very crucial element to your marketing and sales.

As I indicated before, when someone is a prospect and they haven't bought anything from me yet, all I need is an e-mail address. I really don't care about more at that point. I don't need it.

As soon as they buy something, anything at all, for any amount of money, I want to put them into my FileMaker (you can also use ACT!) database. So, Web Marketing Magic handles the database aspect of all of my e-mail addresses. As soon as someone orders something, I then take his or her contact information and I put it into my contact manager, which is called FileMaker Pro.

If you haven't heard of FileMaker before, FileMaker is a software application. It is a contact management software system. It is a terrific product that costs about one hundred fifty dollars, which is relatively inexpensive, and it basically allows you to manipulate your customer data.

I can tell it to give me everybody who bought from me between 1990 and the year 2000 who spent more than $300. You can code information in all different sorts of ways. It's a really cool program and not difficult to use at all. I can use it and if I can use it, anybody can use it because I am not a computer genius at all. I just know how to make money with it; I'm not a computer guy.

I would encourage you to understand that you need to track this information. Another thing that's important is follow up. When you get people's e-mail addresses, immediately follow-up with them the day after you come into contact with them, whether you meet them in person or in a group. Remind them who you are so that when your e-mails start coming along they remember you.

Titling Your Products

Unless you are a well-known celebrity or a well-known entity of any sort, one of the most important elements of creating and selling your information product is a great title. You need a title that exactly describes what the product is and makes people want to buy it. When you title your products, you have to make them compelling. They need to have titles that make people want to jump out of their seats.

The example a lot of marketing gurus use is you have to picture your customer as a sloth-like creature, sitting on their couch, drinking a beer, watching TV, eating bonbons. You have to motivate them off their fat duffs, to get to the phone, put a check in the mail. That really requires a lot of effort on their part, so you better make them sufficiently interested with a sexy title and sexy descriptions of what it is and the great benefits that you're offering in order for them to put any amount of effort into it.

Here's an example of a good title: "Marketing and Promoting Your Own Seminars and Workshops." It's clear and easy to understand what it's about and what the person who buys this program will learn. Years ago I did a 1-day seminar titled: "How to Start and Build a

Consulting Business in Your Own Field." Once again, very clear, simple and easy to understand what the program is all about.

Although it became a massive best-selling book, "What Color is Your Parachute?" is a lousy title. Why? Because you have to work to figure out what the book is about. Originally, it was shelved in the Sports section of the book store. Clerks thought it had something to do with parachuting. It shows you how good the book actually is that it became a massive success with this title. Don't follow this example. It's too much work to try and promote any product with a bad title.

If you're having trouble coming up with a title for your product, use this formula. Pair your USP with the biggest benefit that your product provides to your market. Here's one: "How to Make Your Video Production Business Virtually Immune to Competition."

If you're having trouble, shoot me an email with your idea, but expect an HONEST response from me. Don't do this if you don't like negative feedback.

Pricing Your Products for Maximum Revenue

We need to discuss something called the "Thud Factor" before we talk about specific pricing. When people order stuff from you and give you $500, especially in person, they want to see some bulk. It's like fiber in a diet. They need to see some physical stuff. For example, I have seen people get up in front of groups and pitch something that essentially consisted of handing the group a password. Somehow there's just not a Fudd factor there. They need to have some kind of physical product in their hand to feel as though they were not cheated somehow. In the more techie–oriented community you don't, but in the non-techie community people need to see bulk. Remember that.

Once you understand the Thud Factor, you also need to understand the pricing structure. Many price points can be a combination of multiple products (these are just examples and are not a suggestion of absolutes in terms of pricing - you may have a newsletter you sell for $1000 a month!)

Under $10	Special Reports
$10 - $30	Your Book or e-book
$50	Newsletter
$100	2 Cassette Audio
$200	1 Day seminar
$300	2 Day Seminar
$400	Tele-seminars
$500	Videos
$600	Full Day Seminar on Audio Tape
$700	Coaching Services
$800	Multi-Day Bootcamp
$900	Manuals
$1000	All of the Above
>$1000	High End Consulting

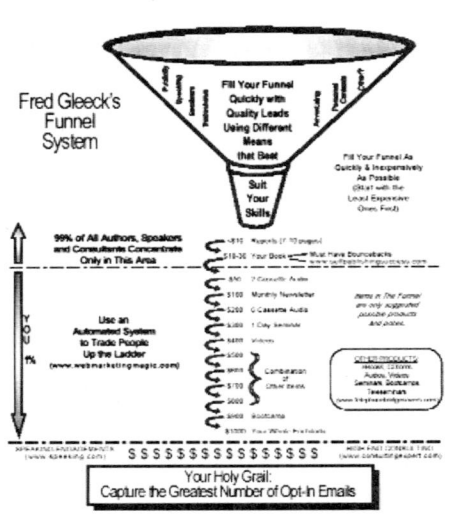

Note:
See page 19 for a larger view of Fred Gleeck's Funnel System.

The VALUE equation

When you start pricing your programs, remember the value equation. Most people price their programs based on what it cost to produce. Wrong. The price of the product should be determined by how much value the product can produce for the user. If you have a product that can make buyers an additional $3,000 in the next 90 days and you can PROVE and GUARANTEE it, then you can consider pricing the product for something below $3,000. How much below $3,000? It depends on your market. After all, even if they pay $3,000 for the thing, after 90 days they would have broken even and the rest of the money from that point on would be gravy.

Here are some general rules of thumb for pricing your info products. If your market can make you more, then by all means sell them at that higher price point. The highest price you will generally charges is 50% of what you can guarantee the product will produce for someone in the first 90 days IF THEY USE IT.

On the low end, set your minimum price to 10% of what the product will produce for them in that same 90 days if they use it. In this case, that would come out to $300. On the high end you would price it at $1500. Since the product can generate someone $3,000 if they use it, 1/10th that amount would be $300 and 1/2 of that amount would be $1500.

The ultimate determination of price will be what price people are willing to pay for it. The above formula is only used to give you a place to start.

Payment Methods: Make it Easy for People to Buy

No matter how good your products are, you'll need to make it easy for people to buy them from you. The more options that you give people, the higher the probability you'll have that you'll sell them something. Make it easy for people to buy.

You want to be able to take checks, checks by fax, etc. You have to expect that a certain number of checks will bounce. Every once in awhile a check bounces. You know what? In the last 16 years that I've been selling informational products, I think I've had maybe 10 checks bounce. Not bad. I've sold about five million dollars worth of stuff myself, so that's not too bad. Ten checks.

If somebody wants to write me a bad check, shame on them. That's really bad karma for them. Somebody doesn't pay for something they got? Bad karma, man. I don't look at that as my problem. That's their problem, not mine. What goes around comes around.

Is there a way of clearing a check before you release the product? Yes. There is a company called Telecheck that guarantees checks. I've never gotten into that because my percentage of bounced checks has been so low I haven't had the inclination to do it. Is there a charge for it? Yes. Have I messed with it? No. Should you? Perhaps. If you're dealing with a mass market and you get a lot of bad checks, it might be a good idea. If you're dealing with a niche market, it is generally not an issue.

Please always take cash. It's a good thing. Money orders are like cash. Take money orders. Take anything they've got. The point is, make it easy for people to buy.

You cannot survive as an information marketer if you don't take credit cards. This is not an optional item. It's mandatory.

The easiest way to set up a merchant account outside of the Web Marketing Manager is to contact a merchant account provider. Start with your local bank for your offline account. If you already have an established relationship with the bank it will be much easier to get a merchant account.

You can also go online using one of the search engines like Google or Yahoo and put in "cheap offline merchant accounts" or words like that. Call them up, ask for references, say, "I've heard there are a lot of scam artists out there."

You will want to have the terminal because you can take the terminal with you and with a cell phone, hook it up remotely. You can be at a trade show and take all kinds of orders for products. Having a physical terminal isn't a bad thing. Do not get screwed, however, by paying some ridiculous amount for that little terminal. I got screwed in the beginning. I paid $1,400 for one of these suckers, which was a ridiculous fee at that time. So do your due diligence, because there are a lot of companies out there that will compete for your business.

I recommend that you have both an online and offline account. If you are doing really big numbers you may want two or three of each. Why? Inevitably there will be a problem and one of your accounts may get shut down. You don't want to lose customers because you can't take their credit cards to order. Let this be the least of your worries.

Testimonials: The "Mother's Milk" of the Product Sales Process

Testimonials are the "Mother's Milk" of the product sales process. This is really critical to selling anything online or offline. You must get testimonials. That's why at the end of every event I do, I ask for testimonials. You don't want "Fred was great. He was a great speaker. He was great." You want "The 7 things that I learned about blah blah will help me make at least $50,000 more next year." The more specifics you can coach people to write when creating a testimonial for you, the better. Specific testimonials become more believable.

Someone will call me and give me great compliments on my products, letting me know exactly what my book has done for the m. I then say, "You know what? That's really great. Would you do me a big favor and put it in writing and fax it to me?" One out of every five people that I beg to do that actually does it. That's why you've got to strike when the iron is hot. You've got to get people to give you testimonials on the spot, when they're thinking of it, when they're there, or in front of you.

It's better if written by hand on their own letterhead. If you can scan in hand-written letters and put them on your web site and go "Click here for all the testimonials" that would even be better. Why? It real. And it's personal. In other words, we now know that you're not making this up. That's important.

Many will want you to write it and have them sign it. In other words, some people are too lazy. They say "Hey you do the testimonial and I'll sign it." The only problem is you do too many of those, and they start to all sound alike. It's actually better if you get your customers to do it as long as you coach them in the process so they give you the specifics. If you actually write it for them, somehow it loses the reality.

It's even better when it's grammatically incorrect. It sounds just like a real human being.

Let's take that a step further. Some will agree to have their phone numbers included. Why would you want this? Let's take a look at some testimonials to answer that.

The worst testimonial:

"It was great. - JR, Omaha, NE"

A step up from that is:

"It was really good. I learned a lot about marketing. - JR, Omaha, NE"

Step up from that is:

"It was really great. I learned the 7 things that I never would have known about marketing from you. - JR, Omaha, NE"

The next step up is:

"It was really great. I learned the 7 things that I should know about marketing from you. - John Rhodes, Omaha, NE."

The next step up would include:

"John Rhodes, Omaha, NE, name of the company."

The next step up would be:

"All that plus his phone number."

If you put phone numbers in testimonials, will they actually get called? Occasionally they will, but very infrequently. If they do, you better make sure you have somebody over on the other end of the phone who agrees to it, number one. Number two, that person had better give you a good recommendation. Number three, if they close any deal for you, you need to send them some kind of a gift. It doesn't have to be big, but you have to first off, call them and thank them, then you have to send them a gift like a gift certificate.

As long as you're in the information marketing business, when anybody says anything nice to you at all, you must capture that data. Remember that.

How do you get them to create testimonials for you? Here are a few tips.

- Evaluations: Make sure to hand out evaluations at the end of any live presentation that you do. Not only will this give you great feedback, but if you do a great job, you'll get some awesome testimonials that you can use anywhere and everywhere.

- Ask for them: When people call you on the phone or send you an email that says: "I loved your product, blah, blah, blah" you need to thank them. After you thank them you need to say: "I'm really glad you got a lot out of it, can I ask you a favor? Would you mind putting that in writing so I can use it in my promotional material?"

- Ask them to fax the quote over to you. Usually they forgot the great quote that they just told you so I tell them I'll write it up and fax it over to them to sign and fax back. That usually works the best. Also, it's less work for them so it's more apt to get done.

- Make sure and archive all of these testimonials. If you use them publicly, the Feds have the right to ask you to produce them at some later point in time.

- The best testimonials are those that come in handwritten. There is nothing more credible than a handwritten letter from a satisfied customer. When you get one of these, always call the people and thank them profusely.

Testimonials in Other Forms

Rick Raddatz, a friend and client of mine, has a site called www.InstantAudio.com. This site allows you to get people to record an audio testimonial and then make that audio file available for people to listen to by clicking a link on your site.

Just as people buy using different modalities of learning, they will also respond to different modalities of testimonials. Providing them with only print testimonials is not nearly as effective as giving them multiple options.

I would encourage you to use both audio AND video testimonials. If you can capture your customers comments in video form, it's big plus. If you're doing a seminar or speech, this would be the ideal time to bring the digital camera with you and capture some laudatory comments from your customers or clients.

Neither the audio or video testimonial need be lengthy to be effective. All you need is a pithy comment that includes specifics about how you helped them to make these work.

NOW, Let's Start SELLING!

Now Start Filling Your Funnel!

Given that your information products business will be web-based, you fill your funnel by sending people to your website. There are two ways to do this: online and offline. You need to do both. Which of the techniques under each method do you use? All of them. But, you have to consider R.O.M.D.

Return on Marketing Dollars (R.O.M.D.)

Every information marketing business succeeds by generating high quality leads at the lowest possible cost. The key to your success in this area is to understand the concept of R.O.M.D. Return on Marketing Dollars. Concentrate on those methods of marketing where you get the greatest possible return for the lowest possible cost.

Not only will you want to do those things which will cost you the least, you'll also want to overlay that with doing those items which best fit your personality.

Simply said: Do things that generate the greatest number of books for the least amount of money but do them in order of what you like to do most or feel most qualified to do.

Writing Copy: Critical whether its copy on your website or anywhere else.

The way you write your sales materials is critical in making your products sell. The main piece of advice that I have for you is to concentrate on benefits, not features. Play up the benefits your clients will receive by purchasing this product, not the features of it. Before going any further, I want to give you some examples of sites to check out.

Take look at www.radiopublicity.com. Alex happens to be among all of the other geniuses and is a very, very good copywriter. Look at www.stopyourdivorce.com. Check out www.amazingformula.com. Or look at some of my sites: www.Consultingexpert.com, www.speeking.com , and www.selfstorage.com.

What I want you to look at specifically when you look at these sites is the quality of the writing and whether or not, after you read it, you feel compelled to buy it, even if you don't need it. That's how good the writing needs to be.

Let's talk about creating this fantastic copy. Most people can't do this on their own, so hire an expert if necessary. If you can do it on your own, that's super. There's a great book by a guy named Jeffrey Lant called Cash Copy. He is very, very bright and knowledgeable and this is a well-written book. If you're feeling brave, call and ask for information on Dr. Jeffrey Lant in Cambridge, MA. He stayed near his alma mater where he graduated summa cum laude. You can call and take some abuse over the phone and he'll send you a book. It doesn't take away from the fact that he writes a great book. Trust me. Try it.

There's also another piece by a guy named Brian Keith Voiles called Ad Magic. Now as opposed to Cash Copy, which will cost you $20 or $30, Ad Magic is a $295 item. It's a big binder on how to write copy. I would advise you to get Cash Copy first.

You can also go to my site: www.WebCopyMagic.com.

You can also look in my Million Dollar Rolodex for a referral. Good copywriters are worth their weight in gold, and can mean the difference between good sales and great sales of your product.

Writing copy is important on your web site, it's important in your catalog, your ads, and anything else that goes to your prospective customers. The writing of the copy is what creates the sale. People don't know what the product is like before they read about it. So you have got to create some great copy in order to make it work. And make it sell.

Designing a Website That Sells: Your website is the HEART of your sales system!

In order to make money online, you have got to design a web site that sells. However, once you have that site, you have to be able to drive traffic there. Let's talk about both of these elements.

There are two primary types of web sites. There's something called a portal site and there's something called a sales letter site. The sites that I just gave you earlier, radiopublicity.com, amazingformula.com, and all of my sites are sales letter sites. They're trying to sell one very specific product or service.

A portal site is something that attempts to be a clearinghouse within a given industry. For example, I'm working with somebody right now, on a ballroom dancing site, in which she's an expert. She's really into ballroom dancing and she wants to take everyone who's interested in ballroom dancing and all the vendors who want to sell to those people, and put the buyer and seller together. So she's going to have a site like ballroomdancing.com. Once you get to her site, you'll see "Click here if you're a vendor or click here, if you're a customer." From that point, you have various options.

Although there are two basic kinds of sites, most of what we're going to be talking about in information marketing really has to do with sales letter sites. Sales letter sites are most effective in getting people to buy things because you're trying to get them to buy one thing and one thing only.

How can you create a good sales letter web site? Look at those who are successful and copy them. How do you judge success? Success is judged based on three things: total amount of the net dollars generated, closing ratio and net value per visitor. Let me give you a description of what these are:

Net dollars - at the end of the year if we knew you did a million dollars in gross sales, and you had $100,000 in expenses, you netted $900,000. We'd have a yardstick to measure you.

Closing ratio - if you closed 8% of the people, we could check that ratio against other people with similar sites or products and see how you compared and that would be important.

Net value per visitor - If you have a digital product (like a PDF file) that sells for $100, it is a no cost item to you. Therefore, in this case, you are making $100 profit with each sale. Let's assume that you get 100 visitors this month and ten people buy the product. Your net dollars for the month is $1000. To figure the net value per visitor, you have to divide the number of visitors into the net dollars. In this case, the average value per visitor is $10. (This is different from the average sale which would be $100).h

Don't try to sell more than one product on a web site unless they know you. Once they know you, you can set up a catalog site in which you offer a whole bunch of stuff. But in general, you want to sell one product per web site. Now that doesn't mean that you can't sell multiple products, but sell them through different web sites. I've got a sales letter web site for every product that I sell! This does not mean that you have to have different web sites for each product. You can have extensions of a web site. For example, you can have seminarexpert.com/salesletter1, seminarexpert.com/salesletter2, etc and have as many extensions as you need. That's a cheaper way to maintain your sites.

I personally have a different domain name for most of my products and that costs me $100 per year per domain. Check out my Million Dollar Rolodex for who to contact for domain names.

You have two goals for the visitors when they come to your site. Buy your low-end e-product or opt into your list. Read this again carefully. Get them to buy your inexpensive digitally delivered front-end product for under 30 or 40 dollars, or opt-in to your list. What's the next option? Go away! We don't want you! Either opt into my list or buy my low-end products or I will see you later.

I have found that it is best to give your visitors the sales pitch before allowing them to opt into your list. This means that they are already a buyer of my products and I can begin upselling them. However, if they choose not to buy, you DO want to capture their email. I do this with a pop-up on exit.

Pop-up on exit means after you've read my entire sales letter and you decided not to buy, I will send a little pop-up screen that will say "Hey, before you go, you can sign up for this free 7-day course on blah blah blah." Don't give them a way to opt-in until they've decided not to buy. You don't want to distract them from your purchase - remember a confused mind always says no!

Driving Traffic to Your Site

Once you have the "perfect" site, you've got to drive traffic there. There are lots of ways to get visitors. Like I said earlier, the two ways are online and offline. Let's go through the techniques to use in each area.

Do you belong to a news group? A news group is where you get on and yak and tell everybody what you think about everything. You need to find news groups by going to search engines and typing in "news groups." Sign up for as many as you can and lurk around in the background before doing any postings. Find out how the newsgroup works and what they talk about. Then go in there and promote yourself. The way that you promote yourself is by getting good information to people. And on the bottom of the good information you put your signature file which gives your name, your site, and a short byline explaining what you do. People who think that your posts are brilliant and intelligent will click on your site. They will decide that you know what is going on and that they want to check out your site to see what you do. This is one way to promote your site and it's free! Remember, though, if you're promoting a karate web site, you don't want to be on a basket weaving news group. It's just not a good match. You want to concentrate in the areas that are relevant in order to generate the business.

Another way to get traffic to your site is through pay per clicks. You can go to www.payperclicksearchengines.com or www.Overture.com, among sixty or more others where you pay per click. The most popular one that I'm using these days is www.google.com.

Here's how it works. You sign up as an advertiser, minimum cost, $25.00. You put this fee on your credit card. After you have signed up, you buy keywords. Keywords are the words people use for a search. For instance, I bought the key words "storage business" at goto.com and when someone enters those words into the search engine, my name will come up as number one for that search term.

Now what's the beauty of pay per click? You don't pay until they click. If someone only searches the term, I do not have to pay. Once someone clicks on my site, I pay per click. For this particular search term, I am paying seven cents a click. You can bid on the search terms and you can decide where you want to rank in the search engine based on how much you're willing to pay.

What does this allow you to do? Let's say your site is www.stopyourdivorce.com. Before you roll out stopyourdivorce.com, you have the web site set up, the copy is written, and you've got the product ready. You go onto goto.com and you enter "relationship advice". You buy a bunch of keywords and you find out how much you're paying for them. If you've got a $100.00 product, that nets $100.00, you will be able to see how much you spend vs. how much you receive and you'll be able to figure out your value per visitor.

Let me give you an example. If I knew that my average value per visitor was $15 and that my cost per click to get people to come to my website was $8, I would do that all day long! That is fifteen dollars in value for eight dollars in cost. I make $7 in the front end and I have a customer for life that I can put in my funnel. Keeping the funnel in mind, in some cases you may even want to break even on the front end. If you can break even on the cost per click and the average customer value, you can fill your funnel for free and have people buy your other products down the line.

The value per visitor will be different depending on where we get them. And so we want to test within each of the means to determine how much we're willing to spend or how much we're willing to give away to get them to become part of our funnel.

The best way to determine what search terms to buy is through research. Put $25 out there in fifty different search engines and find out what your value per customer is with each term. Once you have tested, you know how much you can pay per click.

Auction sites are another clever way to drive people to your site. You can go to Ebay and Yahoo auctions and all these other auctions and set up an account. As a seller of information, you determine a product that you have that you can sell in this way. Even if the people don't buy the product at the auction site, they might go check out my web site (which I am allowed to post as part of my auction description.) It's a good way to get them in the door with a topic and then send them to a web site.

Let's say I go to Yahoo and I look up "publishing" or I go to Ebay and I look up publishing. It will give me a list of everything related to publishing. It's like free advertising to be auctioning something.

You need to know how this works because it's fascinating. If you're not familiar with Ebay, you should pick up a copy of *Ebay for Dummies*. It's a good book, and will teach you how to buy and sell.

You may want to consider search engine placement. It's a very elusive thing. The best way to get better placement in the search engines is to pay someone who is an expert. This is a moving target. What works today may (and probably will not) not work tomorrow. I used to recommend certain people to work with in this area. No more. If you want to find someone, and they are expensive, go to the search engines and put in the key words: "search engine placement." If they can get up to the top in the engines for these terms and they are selling a service that does that exact same thing, chances are they know what they 're doing. Only choose those individual who have gotten good placement in the search engines that are NON paid. Anyone can pay to get placement. That's NOT what we're looking for here.

Search engine experts charge a LOT of money. How much? It depends. Just be sure you're sitting down when you call them. But what they charge is only relative to the amount of money they can generate for you in terms of results. Please make sure you have tested your site to make sure it's selling before you start a search engine placement program. The last thing you want is to get lots of people to your site who then don't buy anything.

Another way is through opt-in names. What does that mean? These are people who have agreed to receive your information via email. They have OPTED to receive your correspondence via email. They have opted-IN. This is another area where people who I once recommended have disappointed me. I would prefer that if you get to the point where you want to try and generate some opt-in names that you call me to get the latest and best contact that I have.

Here's how the concept works. You come up with what is essentially a classified ad for your ezine or list. They run this ad in all kinds of places where people might have an interest in your topic. People then put a check mark in a box (or by NOT checking a box they are agreeing to receive your info) and they are sent an email confirming that they really want to be on your list. This is called a double opt-in system. Absolutely necessary in this era of SPAM and spam laws and regulations. They will continue to run this ad until you have exhausted the amount of money you agreed to spend.

The way it's computed is by the number of names you want to receive. People who sell these kinds of names charge anywhere between 5¢ and 25¢ a name.

I did this last month and got about 1000 names for $200. Now, out of those 1000 names, I have had two sales equaling $200 and therefore, have broken even on my initial investment. I am willing to capture the names through people who sell these names and just break even on the front end. I know that I'll make even more money over time with these folks.

Besides wanting to fill my funnel, do you know another reason that I want to have a large email list? If you are an advertiser, you will want to advertise in my e-zine if I have a large mailing list. These names create on on-going stream of revenue.

Here's a list of some other ways to drive traffic to your site:
- Being involved in clubs, memberships, groups of any type
- Hand out business cards
- Write articles
- Give away free gifts
- Personal contacts

Remember, we can probably construct a hierarchy of value per visitor based on method of getting them to the site. For example, I'll bet that my value per visitor would be highest with personal contacts. In other words, if I'm in here personally telling you "Hey go to this site" your chances of buying will be much higher than someone that I get on a search engine placement or that I pay via a pay per click.

Before you start getting massive numbers of people to go to your website and read your sales copy, you've got to make sure that

Now in terms of marketing philosophy, start with those methods that are the least expensive and match your personal style. We talked about that a little bit earlier. So when you start to fill your funnel with leads, you want to try and do it in the least expensive fashion and in a manner that matches your own personal style. If you like to write, concentrate on writing. If you like to speak, concentrate on speaking. If you like to network, concentrate on networking.

Keep in mind that the greater the level of personal contact you have with people, the higher the probability of getting those people to get on your list. Also, the greater the level of personal contact, the higher the quality of the leads that you generate.

Let me give you a few ideas to start with:

Filling Your Funnel – Offline Methods

In this section I'm going to give you a lot of different ways that you can fill your funnel using offline means to do so. Don't feel you have to do them all. I recommend that you TRY them all. You'll find that certain methods are more successful for you because they match with your skills and personality. Concentrate on those. Now, let's get started!

Trade Shows

Attend industry trade shows in your niche and you can meet prospects face to face. When you attend the trade shows you will first be faced with a choice: get a booth or don't get a booth. Generally booth space is fairly expensive. It may or may not be worth it to rent a booth but you'll only know the answer to that question if you try it.

If you DO get a booth, then you have another choice, you can either try and sell a product to them directly or merely to collect their names and addresses. If you make the decision to sell your information products directly to them at the trade show you'll need to have some way to effectively demonstrate what you're selling. If it's a video, then have a video sample that people can look at.

If you're only collecting names then give people a powerful incentive to have people give them to you. One of the better ideas is to collect all of their pertinent data in exchange for a digitally deliverable product with a high perception of value.

If you decide NOT to get a booth, then make sure that you have GREAT handout piece to put into their hands. This handout can be either for a hard or soft offer or both. Create a one page sheet that offers to sell people a low end product OR offers them a great digital product in exchange for their contact information.

Leads generated at shows will be of fairly high quality. Why? Because you've had the chance to meet with people in person, face to face. Leads that you generate from personal contact will be worth a lot more because people are seeing you in the flesh and you can build a LOT more credibility with them.

Speaking

Anytime you get the opportunity to speak you'll be able to get some very high quality leads into your funnel. The higher the level of personal contact, the greater the chances of generating high quality leads. For more information on how to get speaking engagements take a look at: www.speeking.com.

Seminars

Seminars, similar to speaking engagements allow you to meet with potential customers face to face. You'll be able to impress them with your brilliance on stage or while "schmoozing" in the hallways and get them to either give you their cards (to be input into your funnel manually) or send an email to one of your autoresponders. Seminars are a GREAT place to get high quality leads into your funnel. Like with a speaking event, consider doing a drawing for all those who give you a business card. After the event you can then go back to the office and enter all of the names your database.

For more information on this topic go to either www.seminarexpert.com or www.seminarguru.com.

Personal Contacts

The ultimate method of generating the MOST qualified leads is through one-on-one personal contact. There is no better lead than the guy or gal that you bump into on line at the grocery store. Make sure you always carry promotional material in the form of a business card, flyer or book. But remember, more important than handing out your own promotional material is to GET a business card from someone else.

After you get business cards, immediately follow up with an email to tell people that you were glad to meet them and to suggest to them that they sign up to be on your list.

TeleSeminars

We discussed teleseminars as a product. It is also a great way to fill your funnel. You can invite people who aren't on your list to go to a free or a paid teleseminar. You can use all kinds of means to get people to free teleseminars. One great way is to let some people with large opt-in lists know what you're doing and give them a piece of the action on future sales from the individuals they send your way.

Here's an example. I get 3 people with lists of 10,000 people each to email their list and let them know about an upcoming teleseminar that I'm having. They sign up as an affiliate of mine through webmarketing magic.com. They people who accept get recorded by the system as a lead that they have generated. Their name is "tagged" with this person's identifier.

You can then set up the system to pay your referrer for sales made to their people every time they buy from you. Do you think these 3 people would be excited about sending you people? Absolutely. Particularly if you can prove to them that your lifetime customer value is high. If your LTCV is high (mine is close to $500 per person), then they stand to make a lot of money over time.

Referrals

One of the least expensive ways to get people to your site and thus to buy your information products is through referrals. How do you get referrals? There are a few key ways.

First, you have to make sure you produce GREAT products. If you produce crappy products your chance of getting referrals is virtually nil. As I've mentioned before, this means producing information which is packed with useable content that is relevant and easy to follow and understand.

Secondly, you have to ASK people for referrals. Most people feel squeamish about doing this. They think it makes them look needy. Baloney. Asking for referrals is just good business policy and should be done by everyone, including you.

How and when do you do it? In short, before, during and after the sale. Why is it that few if any people ask for referrals? They are afraid of rejection. The solution? Get over your fear of being rejected and ask for the referrals. If you have a problem with this approach, go talk to an insurance agent and ask them what would happen to their business without referrals. The answer? They'd be dead in the water.

Referrals are one of your least expensive means of generating leads. Ask for them?

Pro-Bono Work

Pro-bono work is where you do work for free. When you do work for free, in certain selected niches you will be doing a good deed and people will get to know you who you are and what you do. As I'm writing this section of the book I'm sitting next to one of the participants who is very active in fundraising for non-profits.

He asked me if I speak at any charity events. I said, absolutely, as long as it's a charity I know, trust and believe in their mission. Can I do this every day of the year? No. I need to make some "real" money as well.

Many of the opportunities that will present themselves from charity events will bear fruit at some point in the future, but it may take a while. If you do this type of work (which I encourage you to do), make sure and choose your causes carefully.

Other People's Seminars or Events

I discussed this earlier in the book and it's a tremendously effective means of generating leads. I think this is a great way to get highly qualified leads and encourage you to re-read that report that you saw early on in the book.

Alumni Associations

Did you go to college or any school that has an alumni association? If so, you should use it to generate high quality inexpensive leads.

Here's my example. I went to the BEST university in the state of Florida, the University of Florida. I also got my graduate degree in International Business from the American Graduate School of International Management. At both of my alma maters I have submitted information that has been published in both of the alumni publications. Do they reach a large number of people? In the case of the University of Florida, yes, in the case of my graduate school, no!

What was the cost to get this information in the publications? Almost nothing. It took me less than 20 minutes to write the letter and toss it in the mail. The result was that both of these publications published my information almost exactly as I sent it to them. What then happened? I got a lot of virtually free, high quality leads from a source where I had an immense amount of credibility.

What's YOUR action point? Get a hold of your alumni office and ask them how you can submit an "update" for their records about you, one of their illustrious former students.

Church Groups

Belong to a church, synagogue, or mosque? If so, you've got another source for inexpensive leads. If you've created an information product, they will probably be willing to give you a mention in their weekly publication or bulletin.

Your key is to getting them to run the address of your website. This will help you to drive high quality leads to your site and then, hopefully, trade them up into buyers of your information products.

Even though the total number of leads you generate may be small (although this may not be true with large churches), the quality of the leads should be very high.

Teach Classes

For many years I taught classes at a number of continuing education organizations in New York City. Although the number of attendees wasn't always stellar, I sold a lot of products and generated some very high quality leads that continue to buy from me many years later.

If you do teach classes, make sure that you are permitted to sell products and capture the names of the attendees for you database. In the event that you're not permitted to do either of the two, take a pass. If you are allowed to do it, then make sure and give people a dynamite class AND record it to have a possible additional product.

There are now a number of places where you can teach teleclasses. Look for the opportunity to do so. The quality of the leads may not be the best, but since the cost is nothing more than your time, do it.

Join Associations

When you join an association you will be cavorting with people who have a similar interest. Generally you should be looking to join associations in two areas. First, in your own field. I belong (reluctantly) to the National Speakers Association. I do a lot of speaking for a living so it makes sense for me to belong to the N.S.A.

I also belong to a number of other associations where my niche market customers attend. In the video production business it's the I.T.V.A. In the self storage industry, it's the Self Storage Association.

You too should join at least two groups. The one where your peers congregate and the one where your prospects "hang out."

As a member of the association of your target market you will be able to have personal contact with people at meetings and other events. This personal contact makes the people you find this way incredibly likely to buy something from you in the future.

Write Articles in Trade Publications

If you want to write articles in trade publications, you should start by calling the editor of the publication. This will be much easier if you already have a book in the field (once again, get that book written!). When I became the author of Secrets of Self-Storage Marketing Success, editors allowed me to write about topics in related fields because I was an "expert." So now, every month, I write a marketing article for the self-storage industry. It gets me lots of leads, lots of back-end funnel business, really high-end feasibility studies, consulting work, etc.

Know the publication and what kinds of articles they publish. Do your homework before you call. If not, you're going to look like a moron. You don't want to call up an editor, tell them that you want to write an article on XYZ and have the editor inform you that they don't write articles on that topic. They are going to realize right away that you have not been reading their publication, and there goes your credibility.

You should be familiar with the issues in the industry, which is why you want to start with your own industry first. When I have branched out into other industries, it's been based on personal contacts - friends I've had or people I've known really well. For instance, I branched out into catering. I had a friend in the restaurant business I knew for years. I also branched out into video production. I had a friend in the video production business. Those different sites were the result of my knowledge of an industry, either direct knowledge or tangentially through a friend. I can go into a new industry because I love the content, but before I begin writing articles, I will interview a whole bunch of experts and get to know what it is all about.

When you contact the editor, you need to have sample articles ready to send via e-mail. If the editor says, "Yes. I'd like to see something you've written," you don't want to make them wait. You must be able to send something immediately. If you have a sample article ready to go, you'll impress them with your preparation and they'll be much more likely to read your material.

Payment in an industry trade publication is generally not going to be in actual cash. Sometimes they will pay people who are outside the industry for articles, but for those inside, the only payment you'll receive is the bounce back on your by-line. If they don't give you a bounce back for the byline, you don't write the article. I use my 800 number and I put in an email for them to contact. I will not give my web site because, remember, I want to capture their email address. A sample byline might go something like this:

> *"If you enjoyed this article and want to get the 7-day free course on marketing your own seminars and workshops, send an e-mail to tips@seminarexpert.com."*

Advertising

Advertising is something that you have to pay for. I'd prefer you concentrate on exhausting all of your non paid means of filling your funnel before you move to the paid method.

Generating leads into your funnel via advertising can be effective but is also costly. The quality of the leads is much lower than any lead you generate through personal contact. It can still be effective if you find a way to do "self liquidating" ads. These are ads that end up costing you nothing because there is enough revenue generated on the front end to pay for the ads. My best example is the ads I used to run in the self storage magazines that got people to request a $10 audiotape. Enough people gave me $10 to pay for the $1200 ad. Many of the 120+ people who bought the audio tape went on to buy other products and services.

Space Ads

Space advertising generally only works within your niche market. I wouldn't do space ads in publications that aren't niched. It's a waste of money, and a waste of effort. Additionally, I would start with a very small space ad.

This ad is not for information alone. The goal of the space ad is to get a RESPONSE! You should give people multiple means of response in a space ad - either call me, write me or e-mail me. Give them all the different options because just like with different modalities of learning, some people like different methods of contact.

When you do a space ad, you need to make it self-liquidating. What does that mean? A self-liquidating ad pays for itself on the front end. In other words, if we have a small space ad that's costing us $300 a month, we want to make sure that we make at least $300 a month on the front-end even if we capture an additional two to three hundred e-mails a month. If you don't do this, you are going to have cash flow problems. If you place an ad that is self-liquidating, by all means, place another one in the same publication. If you are making money on the front-end, you definitely continue! In fact, you may want to consider running a bigger ad or an additional ad. If, however, an ad was placed for a month and was not self-liquidating, don't place another!

In order to make the ad self-liquidating, you have to decide on a front-end product. I primarily use seminars. You might use a book. The reason why I use seminars as front-end products is because the information found in the seminars are all my own ideas. I love speaking. I want to do only what I love. I want you to only do what you love.

I no longer write my own books, I hate to tell you that. I don't have the time. I don't like the writing process, so I take my manuscript that

I've knocked out or I take a transcription of a seminar and I get a book written. Take a look at my Million Dollar Rolodex for who I use for ghostwriting and editing.

If you love to write, then please write. If you don't do writing, then find a clever and creative way to create written material. Remember, it is essential to have written material, particularly a book, to be seen as credible.

Advertising itself will attract consulting business. Consider this consulting business as gravy. I get calls once a week from people who see my ad in the storage industry who want to use me as a consultant who have never bought a single product of mine.

Classified Ads

Classified ads are a good place to test because they're cheap. You can also put them in a lot of publications quickly and easily. Be sure to code them so that you know whether or not they're working.

The strength of your copy is key to your success. How you write your ad copy will determine how well the ad does. Remember, people take action based on your copy before they've received the product. The headline is the single most important part of your ad. Make your headlines a stand-alone sentence.

You could put "How to Sell and Publish Your Own Book, Get Famous and Make $250,000 a Year" and then put "Free Info, tips and blah blah blah". You also need to have your 800 number and an email address to respond to. Be sure to give them multiple means of response. You've got to make it as simple as possible while saying the essence of what people need to hear. Another example of a headline is "How to Get Your Own Radio Show in 7 Days or Less". It says it all and it really identifies what you're going after.

There are national organizations that will place your ad in a selection (of your choosing) of newspapers at one time. The beauty of some of these papers is that they are out in the middle of nowhere in the weekly publications, and you don't have access to those publications yourself. The cost per unit to capture the names is really low. They might be charging you three dollars a week to run a classified ad. So it might be worth looking at. But, first off, start out by testing your own copy locally by running classifieds in your local papers.

Now to be honest, I don't have the names of those national organizations because I haven't used them. If you are interested in that concept, go into the search engines and put in "national classified advertising". These companies will put your ads into these papers for a fee, which will keep you from having to call each and every one of them yourself.

Direct Mail

Given the amount of email that everyone gets these days, it may surprise you to know that direct mail effectiveness is actually increasing if you do it right. There are two basic types of direct mail I want to talk about here.

Sales Letters

Sales letters are anything that you get in the mail that comes in an envelope and contains and offer in writing. These letters can come in a variety of forms. They can be normal #10 envelopes or they can come in unusual funny colored envelopes.

Why spend the money to send a big letter to people just to get them into their funnel? If the value of the lead that you generate is sufficiently large enough, it may be well worth it to use this method of generating leads.

Writing an effective sales letter is a book in itself. If you want to find out how to write the most effective direct mail piece, pick up one of the many books by my good friend, Bob Bly. Just go on Amazon, put in his name and you'll find a ton of books that he's written.

A good friend of mine, Kirt Christensen, a well-known internet marketer, has been successfully using sales letters after he gets his large email list to respond to an offer for a free downloadable audio program. Those who opt for that package are required to give him their full address. He then follows up with those folks with a sales letter. He's had success using this system and I suggest you try it as well.

Get people on your email list to agree to get a free product (with good value) in exchange for providing all of their physical address details. Then follow up with a sales letter to sell these folks on a high priced product related to what they just got for free.

Postcards

Postcards are the one of the only method of traditional direct marketing that's still affordable because postcards are inexpensive to mail. The beauty about a postcard is that you can direct the prospects to a pre-recorded message or send them to an e-mail address. Additionally, when they arrive at the door, they're already opened. Your prospective customer doesn't have to open an envelope.

Remember, your goal with prospects is to get them to take one specific action. You want them to either call or fax or send an email. You don't have a lot of room on a postcard, so don't try to do more than get them to take that one action.

For example, if I was doing a pitch for an event, I would say "If you're interested in marketing information products, you need to find out about how to blah blah blah and get filthy rich, click on this or go to this link. And, so they go to the link and it would be a description of this seminar, a very lengthy description, trying to get them to sign up for the seminar. That's how I would do it.

The beautiful thing about a postcard is, even if you have a fairly long link, they have the postcard there in front of them so they can type it in; it's not like they have to remember it. If for instance, you directed people to www.selfpublishingsuccess.com, they would be able to get that into their computer rather easily. On the radio or an event where they can't write it down or look at it you want to give them something easy!

A great way to maximize the effectiveness of a postcard campaign is to get a hold of a list from an association where you sell products. Many of these lists are compiled by people who join the associations and then pay someone to enter the entire list of names into a database. Just make sure that you're not violating any rules of the association when you do this if you don't want to rock the boat.

You will now have a lot of their e-mail addresses and all their physical addresses. I don't believe in stamps, although I have to buy one every once in awhile. If you don't believe in stamping, what you can do is you can take that membership list, send them all a postcard, make them an outrageous offer and seduce them into getting into your funnel. This gives you their email address, and voila, no more stamps!

Let me walk you through this: Say you have a list of 3,000 people from an organization. Send out a postcard to each one of them. Postage for each postcard is 21 cents and the entire mailing including labeling, the cost of the postcards, etc. will cost you about 30 cents a piece. Use a basic cardstock postcard, preferably one that is a bright obnoxious color. Remember, to get the twenty-one cent rate on the postcard, it's got to be a small postcard. There is a certain height and length requirement and if you exceed that, you will get all of your postcards returned by the post office as oversized. Keeping to the smaller sized postcard, this entire mailing will cost you $750.

You are looking to capture email addresses and to break even on the front end. Don't worry about the future cash flow for now. You're going to seduce them to go to a web page and make them an offer for an inexpensive front-end product (or perhaps even a free product). If they don't buy it, there will be a pop-up menu that says, "Wait a second! Don't leave yet! Sign up for Fred's free tips!" So, if I can't get them on the front-end product, I'll try to capture at least their email.

Let's look at this carefully. If your product is $30 digital product (a PDF file), how many people do you need to break even? You need 25 people to order the product. Hopefully you can get at least 25 people and you're hoping you can get at least two or three hundred people to sign up for the free tips. Once you get these people into your funnel you begin sending them auto responder messages to get them to buy the book they didn't want to buy at the web site! But you're going to show them how brilliant you are with all your content ideas and dazzle them with that and then you're going to try to get them to buy the front-end product.

It's possible to sell low-end products with the postcard alone to a new prospect. A better way to do this is to get the people you mail postcards to call a free recorded message that tells them why it's a good idea for them to go to the website and either buy or collect a downloadable product for free.

With existing customers who have already purchased from you, it is possible to get those people to buy just from a postcard alone. For example, people come to my seminars as a result of a postcard mailer, even though it's a $97 product. I can only do that with people who are previous customers of mine. I couldn't send a simple postcard mailer unless I had name-brand recognition in the marketplace because people wouldn't go for it.

When I do postcard mailings, I make them wild, bright neon colors. I either do fuchsia, green, or yellow. When you open your mailbox, I want you to go "What the hell is this?" I want to get your attention.

Make sure that when you're sending out the postcard that you consider using the address correction feature to clean your list. Try and clean the list often so you don't waste postage.

TV Advertising

TV advertising is expensive and can be a very DANGEROUS way to fill your funnel. Again, the best and most effective use of television for the information marketer has been to fill seminar seats. You've surely seen the 30 or 60 second spots that promote an upcoming "preview" seminar at your various local hotels. If you haven't, you either don't watch a lot of late night TV or you live in a smaller market that is ignored by this group.

When you get to the point where you're even considering TV, get in touch with me before you blow a big wad of cash. Trust me, I've done it and show you the pitfalls to avoid. In the next section I have given you an idea of how to use an infomercial. They have been used very effectively for many years to sell info-products.

Infomercials

Infomercials are a means of actually selling a product and also for useful in getting name-brand recognition out there. I did an infomercial about 15 years ago. I had one of the first ones on the air, back in 1985-86.

There are two basic types. The traditional form is the 15-minute, or 30 minute or 60 minute spot where you show your product, what it can do, have testimonials, etc. The term "infomercial" has now been used for what's called "short form" like 60-second and 120-second spots. In other words, where they're selling a product on a 1-minute or 2-minute commercial.

The best and most effective use of the infomercial for information products has been Carlton Sheets, the real estate guru and Tony Robbins who does the Personal Power training. Both of them have successfully sold their front end info-products via infomercials and have become household names. Many others have failed and lost millions of dollars. This is a very difficult and expensive game to play, but some people have hit the jackpot.

Leads can be generated for info-products through what's called PI, which is a "pure inquiry" ad. What happens in a pure inquiry situation is you don't pay for the advertising time. You only pay when a product is sold. In other words, if your products cost $30, you don't pay any money for the advertising, but they only pay you $6 an order. Well, who cares if you got a good back-end, you're making six bucks profit from having to put no risk out. It's a great deal for you. And as long as you have some bounce back offers in there and some upsells in there, you've got some great potential.

I may work with a guy who has got an interesting product on the market. He developed this little plastic overlay that goes over a computer keyboard, so that when you put it on the keyboard, you never look down and your keys are always in the right place and you don't make as many typing errors. You can type 40-50 times faster with using this device as a training tool. You can get kids to type faster, you can get adults to type faster, you can get everybody to type faster. Cost and manufacturing on this product is two dollars. We're going to sell it for $29.95. We're going to have an infomercial running all over the place. We're going to test the cheap infomercial first and then roll it out.

Are we going to brand this product? Yes, but we're going to brand it at way above break-even. We're going to make a ton of money on the front-end branding this product. Then, when we've made all our money on the front-end, what are we going to do? We're going stick it in all the retail stores. We'll take it to Wal-Mart, K-Mart, Best Buy and everywhere else.

For those of you reading this book right now, infomercials are probably not relevant at this point. If you have infomercial questions, you can call me at my 800 number, 1-800-FGLEECK, that's 1-800-345-3325.

Radio Advertising

If you're operating on a limited budget, chances are you will NOT be doing any radio advertising to fill your funnel for your info-products. If your budget is fairly substantial and you're promoting a seminar, it MAY be worth while to test this medium.

Work with a professional direct marketer who has experience in this area to write an effective ad (feel free to call me for a recommendation).

Whatever you do don't believe the line of bull about how you must run an ad repeatedly to get it to work. This is a line they feed uninformed marketers to get them to spend more money. If you run an ad once and it doesn't pull, it's certain that you either have a bad ad, OR, that radio won't work for you. The only way to know, if you are running radio ads is to try and tweak the ad to see if you can increase response rates. If you do that and you still don't get results, save your money and don't bank on radio to drive people into your funnel.

Publicity

Getting publicity is a great way to drive traffic to your site. The beauty of this method is that it's perceived as an endorsement when a newspaper writes an article about you and/or your products or a radio station has you on as a guest.

Radio

The entire topic of radio publicity is much better handled by my friend, Alex Carroll. His site is www.radiopublicity.com. I highly recommend that you go there. If you buy anything, make sure you tell him that I sent you!

Print

The master of print, and for that matter, all forms of publicity is Paul Hartunian. A good friend of mine who is also a big dog lover, like myself. Paul is the guy who sold the Brooklyn Bridge.
To learn more about how to generate ALL forms of publicity, go to www.Hartunian.com. Again, please tell Paul that I sent you.

Selling Products from the Platform

There are only a few things that I do really well in life and this is one of them. For some reason I've developed a knack for selling products when I'm up in front of people at an event. Selling products on the platform is when you get up in front of a group of people at a seminar or event and you pitch them on your products or services. For the first public seminar I ever did back in 1984, I had products to sell. I've been doing it for quite a while. In addition to that, I'm obsessed with doing it well. I analyze what I do every time to see how I can improve.

I'll give you a quick summary here, but this is another area where I have written a book that goes into this topic in incredible depth and detail. I highly recommend it. It's called Selling Products from the Platform. You can get a copy of my ebook at www.sellingproducts-fromtheplatform.com I really don't publicize this book because it's a very niche-specific book. It's very niched to the speaking market, but I am going to take that book, as I have with all of my other books, and create a real physical booklet.

If you like doing seminars and speaking, this can be a great sales outlet. For those who sell information products, your revenue will be divided up into about six different categories:

1. Speaking
2. Seminars
3. Coaching
4. Consulting
5. Web Sites
6. Products

I sell 50% or more of the products I sell from the platform – at an event. For example, when I go to an event and there are 150 people there, I can sell as much as l $20,000 worth of stuff. Platform selling is one of my primary means of selling products. I can do this at my own events or at other people's.

The key is to have products that you believe in. Here's one of the funniest things I've ever seen. You get people who say "Well, I don't think it's very professional to try and sell products from the platform." And do you know what I want to say to them? I want to look at them and say, "Because you and your products SUCK!" If your products suck you should be embarrassed. You shouldn't consider it professional. If you've got great products, you should get up there with the zeal of a Baptist preacher. I mean, if you've got good stuff, you should get people, grab them by the scruff of the neck and go "Hey. Pull out your credit card and buy this stuff!"

Every once in a while I get this comment. "Well, why don't you just give us the stuff for free?" And I say, "What are you ... nuts?" I say "Number one: This is a capitalist society. Number two: Even if I wanted to, the people who got the stuff wouldn't place any value on it". You've got to have some dollar amount associated with the purchase or else people don't pay attention to the product. They won't value it unless they have to pay for it. This is a fact.

If you've got good products, every time you stand up in front of a group I want you to tell people to reach into their wallet and give you money. It's going to help them. If you really have developed material that is ten times in value what you charge for the stuff, you should have no hesitation getting people to get out their money and give you some of it. It's not wrong at all. If you buy my products, you buy my materials, you come to my event, I will save you hundreds of hours of time. I never have any doubt of that. That's why when you see me pitch my products, I'm strong, I'm confident and I believe in what I'm selling.

If you've got lousy products people are going to smell it. They're going to smell your insincerity; they're going to smell the baloney. They can tell. When someone tells me they're having a problem selling products, I say, "How good do you think your products are?" And they'll tell me "Well, they're pretty good." I say, "They're pretty good?" How do you feel if you buy something that's pretty good? You better feel like if you buy something it's great. You should want to shout it from the rafters how great it is. If you can't produce a product like that then go back and redo your products." I agree - don't sell your products if they stink. The single biggest key to selling products from the platform is having products that are great.

In my book, I list a lot of things that you must do to be successful, but here are my top 5:

- First, you have to have products that you think are worth 10 times what you're asking people to pay for them. If your products aren't GREAT, don't expect to be successful asking people to buy them.

- Second, you have delivered a lot of highly useable content in the presentation itself. Great content is essential.

- You've got to feel your products will make a significant change in people's lives. That there's a real benefit to them if they buy your product.

- You have to offer products that you're proud of – both from a packaging and a content standpoint. If you don't believe in them, no one else will either.

- You must attack conventional wisdom. If people perceive that your products are not new and innovative, they'll have no reason to purchase them. They'll think there's nothing new under the sun. You have to convince them that your products are new and exciting and contain information they haven't seen before.

Online Ways to Fill Your Funnel

Let's cover some of the means of filling your funnel using online means. Those items that have been covered earlier in this book I'll only give a brief mention to. If you want to get more information about this topic, take a look at one of my other books: "How to Double Your Sales on the Web in 90 Days or Less."

Banner Ads

Banner ads used to be a very popular way to drive traffic to sites. Not anymore. Most of them don't work, Don't ignore them though because for the right price (a very low price), they might. It's worth a test.

Go to a site that is already attracting the kind of people you're targeting. See if they already have banner ads on their site. If they do, ask them if they will let you test a banner on a pay-per-click basis. Talk to your webmaster to figure out the technical details of how to do this.

Chances are they may want you to pay by the number of impressions rather than on a pay per click basis. Either way, throw a few hundred dollars at it and, using the adtracker from WebMarketingMagic, see if the numbers work. Remember to compute not just your front end sales but how much your customer will be worth to you on a lifetime basis. NEVER spend more than you can make back on the front end to get leads. You'll quickly go broke doing that!

Co-Registration Names

Have you ever gone to a site to buy or sign up for something and after you signed up they gave you a list of OTHER people's ezines that you can join? Usually there a number of options where you can check (or uncheck) a clickbox to "opt-in" to a list.

Many of the names you get through this method are fairly useless, BUT, remember to look at the numbers. If you pay $1,0000 to get 50,000 of these names, then all you have to generate lifetime to make them worthwhile is $1,000. Don't worry about response rates.

I've worked with a few people who do co-registration. I can't recommend any of them. If you want to find a source for these kind of names, put in the words "co-registration" or "co-reg" in a search engine and start looking around. Be careful, my experience with these folks has been less than stellar. This doesn't mean you shouldn't do it, just be cautious.

I know a number of people who have been successful with "co-reg" names. Since they are generally low quality names, you may need to use a 2 step approach. Get these names to respond to an inexpensive offer and then PHYSICALLY send them a direct mail piece to promote a more expensive related product. You'll obviously want to capture their physical addresses to make this possible.

Be careful of the new "Can-Spam" laws. Make sure you can prove that someone signed up to be on your list and be prepared to produce this information if you're ever asked. To find out more about this topic, go see my buddy Shawn Casey. He's a lawyer and a very talented information marketer. You can find his program on how to navigate the laws effectively at shawn@mininggold.com

Linking Strategies

Getting people to link to your site is a great way to get free traffic. And, for that matter, get better listings in the search engines. I always love it when people link to my sites, but I don't like to reciprocate. Here's why.

I don't want anyone who comes to my site to have a reason to leave the site before they buy anything. Your primary mission when they visit your site is to sell them a front end product. Don't let them go off onto the wild blue internet until they do so.

Instead, have a link page with all of the links that people will only give you if you link back to them. This page can be "hidden" in your site so that people won't be distracted from what you want them to do which is BUY!
Getting a lot of people to link to your site will improve your ratings in the search engines assuming everything else being equal.

Newsgroups

Newsgroups are where people who have similar interests get together to "chat" about what's going on their industry or topic area. It's an ongoing, virtual trade show for those who have an interest in a given topic.

There are online groups for virtually anything you can imagine. If you can believe it, I had a client years ago who was a RABBIT BREEDER. This area has 4 trade magazines devoted to it, so there's probably a group that will meet your needs as well.

The first thing you'll need to do is find the groups. They are most easily found by going to the major search engines like yahoo and google. The search engines themselves host some of these groups. At yahoo, you'll find a listing of all kinds of groups by going to group.yahoo.com. Don't put the "www" in front of this address.

You'll find a similar list of these groups at google. To find that one, go to www.google.com and do a search using the key words: "google groups." This will get you there. The web address is so long I'd rather not confuse you here by giving you the long and complicated address.

Want to find even more groups? Once you get involved with a group, you can start asking people for other groups that they know of. They'll be happy to give you a list of every group that they're a member of.

Now that you've found the groups and joined, here's your next step: LURK! What is "lurking"? It's pretty much just what it sounds like. Hang out and watch what goes on before you start participating. This will ensure that you don't make some big blunder and have everyone start screaming at you online. I've had it done to me and it's not pleasant.

On the other hand, you may want to get people all riled up at some point intentionally. I just want you to make sure you know the rules of the game before you start.

Before you get going, remember what your goal is: to drive traffic to your site. This can be accomplished by giving people good advice and then giving people a way to find out more about you by listing your web address. Let me elaborate.

When a discussion arises about a topic where you have expertise, watch how things go for a while. When you do contribute make an insightful comment that hasn't been given on the topic and explain your reasoning in a rational manner. Unless you're intentionally trying to rabble rouse, don't be politically incorrect or ill-mannered.

Once you give your brilliant comment, include what's called your signature file at the end of your email. This consists of your name, your USP, your offer and how they can respond.

Here's an example:

Fred Gleeck
Author of 11 books including:
Marketing and Promoting Your Own Seminars
and *Workshops and Publishing for Maximum Profit.*
www.seminarexpert.com
To get your 7 day free ecourse (normally $37)
send a blank email to tips@seminarexpert.com

To analyze this "sig" file, let's take a look. First, you want to put your name, your credentials as they relate to that particular group, your web address and your "soft offer." A soft offer isn't a blatant sales pitch. It's giving someone something free so that you can sell them something later.

Make sure that every time you make a comment that you back it up with DATA. Preferably well-researched data. Don't have data? Get some. Take a survey of a group of people and get their feedback on an issue. Does it have to be a scientific survey? It would be better if it was, but it isn't mandatory. Just make sure that when you volunteer information and advice that people feel that you've got some valid data to stand on.

These groups are filled with politics and agendas by the members. I can't believe how childishly adults can behave in these groups, but they DO! Unless you're intentionally trying to stir the pot you'll want to follow the rules of the group. Don't fight back when others attack you. Let those who agree with you defend you.

All of this being said, I have a hard time sticking to these rules. I sort of like controversy and have created a hard core group of followers who like my "in your face" "no-spin" approach. I've also got a lot of detractors. But remember the saying that I've coined: "Unless a quarter of the people think you're crazy, you're probably not speaking the truth."

Use newsgroups to get the word out about your site and drive traffic to it. Just understand the rules of the game.

Join a Community

There are a number of places online where people can get together and "chat" about a specific topic. Whether it's Ping-Pong or Home Schooling, there's a place online where people get together to shoot the breeze and discuss issues of interest to everyone in that field.

The two most popular places to find these are at Google and Yahoo. Both of them have groups that you can join, post great answers to questions and put your signature file along with your post for all to see.

Auction Sites

Ebay and other auction sites are great for getting people into your funnel. A lot of people go to Ebay every day. It's one of the most trafficked sites on the web. There are probably plenty of your potential customers who are going to Ebay that you could tap.

Look at auction sites as a way to generate leads at negative cost. If you sell an audio program for $19 or $29 on your topic you'll get a whole lot more buyers than at a higher price point. But who cares, you now have the name of a very qualified person who has actually paid money to buy something. It's a good chance they will pay money to get more if you do a good job with the first one.

This is the same reason I sell things on Amazon. A lot of people are shopping there. If you aren't selling on Ebay, get with the program.

Search Engine Optimization

I talked about this in an earlier section as well.

Getting yourself great placement in the search engines without paying for it is an elusive goal. As soon as you learn how it works, the rules are inevitably changed. A lot of people out there claim they can help you get top rankings and a lot of them are crooks. Be careful.

If you're a real techie you might try and figure this stuff out yourself, but my advice is to leave it to the professionals. The question is then: which professionals? The answer? Ask them for multiple references and some kind of performance contract that makes their compensation contingent upon results. If they won't give you both of these, take a pass.

If you can get your site indexed high in the major search engines like Google and Yahoo you'll get a boatload of traffic.

Talk to my webmaster, Phil Huff to get his best, most recent opinion on the subject. He's at www.PhilHuff.com.

Write Articles in E-Zines

Writing articles for e-zines is similar to writing for trade publications. How do you find out where the e-zines are? There's a place called lifestylespub.com. They sell a $39 listing or book of all of the e-zines that are out there, and they separate them by category. It gives all the information about the e-zine: who to contact, whether they take articles from outside sources, etc. It's a great resource in getting your e-zines articles out there.

Some of these e-zines have three, four, five thousand members or subscribers. They'll let you write the article and then at the end you can put a link and tell them about your site and boom! You get all these people coming over to sign up for your free stuff so that you can get them into your funnel. It's a great way to do it and it's free, if you like to write.

To find a listing of ezines, go to www.ezinedirectory.com.

Buying Exit Traffic

Another rather advanced technique to generate cheap funnel traffic is to buy traffic from people leaving other sites. Again, this being a rather technical procedure, leave it to your webmaster, but by all means, look into it.

Here's how it goes. People visit a site where you surmise that those people might be good prospects for your products and/or services. When they leave that site (without buying) they are directed to your website. You then have the possibility of selling them something or capturing their email address for future sales.

The traffic that they generated at the other site cost money to get there. Whether it was pay-per-click or some other method, there were costs associated with getting the people there. Offering the owners of the site compensation for people who leave without buying is subsidizing their cost of generating leads and traffic.

You're buying "used" traffic, you can usually get it pretty cheap and the people who sell it to you recoup some of their costs of getting it to their site in the first place.

The problem with this system is that it makes sense but many people don't get it. If you can understand the system yourself and explain it properly to your target market they may bite. What's it worth to do this? You have to test. Let's say that the primary site is paying $1.00 a click to get people to the site. A good place to start would be 10¢ for every visitor that they send to you. They cut their costs by 10% and you've got cheap traffic in the field that you're looking for.

This isn't a technique that you'll use a lot, but it's good for you to know about it.

Joint Ventures

A very powerful way to get leads and make sales online is through joint ventures. Joint ventures come in various forms, but the most common involves approaching another person who has a list of people you would like to get to. You work out a deal to have that person make an offer to their list and you split the profits.

What is the split? It all depends. If you are dealing with a very well known, highly successful marketer, you may end up giving them the entire front end. So, if you're promoting a $100 product, you let them keep all of the profit (be sure to let them know your product cost and subtract that amount out so you don't get screwed).

Joint ventures can be done both on and offline. When they are done online it involves having someone send someone to your site with a code attached (this can be done by WebMarketingMagic). If they buy, the Joint Venture partner is then given the split that you decide on if and when they order the product.

It's important that your site has a good conversion ratio so that your joint venture partner doesn't waste a selling opportunity to their list. The worst thing you can do is to get your JV partner to mail to a list of 100,000 people and have it only produce 2 orders.

People with lists hate to do an offer that doesn't bear fruit because they can only go their list on occasion. You can't go to them every few days. The JV partner will be looking to know your conversion ratios before they even consider a deal with you. Make sure you can produce these numbers for them or you'll look foolish.

Here's a recent example of JV I'm doing. A guy named Brett Ridgeway is a friend and is also involved with helping seminar promoters sell their products at the back of the room. Brett will go to a seminar and basically take over the sales process and merchant processing in exchange for a percentage of the gross.

While talking one day we were trying to come up with a product to sell to people who he attend seminars where his is handling the back of the room sales function. What we came up with is a product for people who want to speak at other people's seminars. How many times have you been at a seminar and thought you could do a better job than the person that was on stage? My guess? A number of times.

This program shows you how to do that.

Since I don't go to all the seminars that Brett does, we decided to create this product together. We will split the revenue, he will produce and fulfill it and I will get a cut on any sales that he makes. We both will own the names of the people who buy this program.

I intentionally structured this deal to give Brett a larger share than I made on this product. Why? So that he would be encouraged to sell it and it would generate me great quality leads that I can sell other products and services to. The proverbial win-win deal.

Affiliates

Affiliates are your straight commission sales reps on the internet. The more affiliates you can attract, the better. It doesn't matter if someone sells anything or not because you only pay them when they do. Affiliates (using WebMarketingMagic) can sign up to sell your products and services. After they sign up they will get a coded link. When they send someone to your site and they buy, you get a piece of the action. That piece should detailed for your affiliates in advance to let them know what they're making.

The most important thing you can do for your affiliates is to make sure that you've got a site that is converting well. If your site doesn't convert well people will get really ticked off sending you all of their traffic in exchange for NO orders.

You'll also want to provide your affiliates with sales and marketing tools to help them better sell your products and services. I suggest you sign up for a few of the top internet marketers affiliate programs to see how the sharp guys do it.

Sign up with: Armand Morin: www.gogenerator.com; and Yanik Silver: www.surefiremarketing.com . Take what they do and "borrow"from it.

Giving your "people" these tools won't guarantee their success, but it will give them the best chance. No matter how good your conversion rate, it won't matter if your affiliates can't get people to visit the site. You've done your part if you've got a website that sells effectively and you've given your affiliates the tools to be successful.

In most businesses you'd have to be concerned about who you recruited to sell for you. Not here. Naturally, you want the best people working with you but it doesn't matter if you have some dead weight. They get all the tools and then do nothing with them.

To get people to really make you some money, hold contests. Give people incentives to sell. Offer training for them. Anything and everything you can do that will help should be done.

The most effective recruitment system for finding affiliates is to put in your key words and find those people who show up at the top of the search engines. When you find those folks, approach them to become your affiliate. Remember that people at this level will want to know your numbers, so be prepared for some very pointed questions as to your conversion ratios and average visitor value.

Type-In Traffic

I've talked about it earlier in the book but this topic bears repeating. You can reserve domain names for under $10 if you go to www.ultra-cheapdomains.com. Try and reserve a few common misspellings of words or phrases that relate to your topics and "dotcom them."

I'm sitting right next to my good friend and coaching client, Scott Hove as I write this section of the book. He told me that last night he reserved the site: www.catlovergift.com. He found out that last month it got 47,000 people who searched for this term in Overture, one of the paid search engines. The theory is that if people are searching using these terms it is highly probable that people will go online and put in the same words and assume there is a .com associated with the phrase.

You can do the same by going to: inventory.overture.com. Do NOT put in the "www" in front of this string. You'll find the search suggestion tool. Input the key words that you think that people will be using to search for something in your niche and you'll get the results of how many people that month in Overture. Many people spend a lot of time using this tool searching for untapped niches. They ARE out there if you look.

Even if you get one person of the course of the next year to buy one product reserving domains this way it will pay for itself. As I mentioned earlier, I own www.speeking.com. I also own www.puvlishing.com as well as www.FredGleek.com . My name is correctly spelled with a "C" before the "K" but this incorrect spelling gets LOTS of type-in traffic.

Most people, once they hear this, have a tendency to go kind of nuts and start buying a boatload of domains. My suggestion is be aggressive but be prudent. Also, only buy them for a year at a time, attach an ad-tracker to them and if they don't pull their weight – drop them.

Write a Book

We talked about this in detail earlier in the book. Write a book and you'll have a way to generate leads into your funnel and get paid for it. Make sure you've got powerful bounceback offers all over the place to make sure that it happens.

Selling via Amazon

Every information product producer should be selling their products on Amazon. People mainly use Amazon to look for books but I've sold a TON of other materials via Amazon. Here's how you do it. Go to Amazon and click on the link to their advantage program: www.amazon.com/advantage.

This program allows you sell books and other information products through the largest book seller in the world. When people are interested in information about a given topic, many of them will go to Amazon to see if a book exists. Even if they don't find a book, they might find your videos or audio programs.

To get listed in the program every product you sell must have an ISBN numbers. If you're thinking of creating a slew of products you may want to rethink the idea of only getting 10 of them to start. I got 100 when I first got going and I've burned through all of them. If something is going to be sold on Amazon is MUST have an ISBN number. This is not optional.

Books, audios and videos all use the same ISBN numbers.

People often use Amazon as a search engine, so your titles become crucial. Here's an example. I've got a program called: "24 Secrets to Radically Improve Customer Service." I sell these videos for $99 each. This means that Amazon gives me about $45 for each one (45% of the gross amount). I put this video together a long time ago. I still sell 3 or 4 of these each month with NO marketing whatsoever. My original cost to produce this video was under $3500. I've made that money back many times over before I even started selling it on Amazon.

This is FREE money. All I have to do is get copies of the video made, shrink wrap them and put the ISBN number sticker on the outside. I don't have a fancy box or anything. People buy them because the search by the term "customer service" and find my video. It doesn't even have a picture of the product and barely has a description. All you need is to have about 20 or 30 of these kinds of videos on Amazon that sell at a decent clip and you can send your kids to college. What a country!

Not long ago I had a customer order my book: "Secrets of Self Storage Marketing Success" through Amazon. About two weeks after ordering, they faxed in an order sheet I put in the back of that book with an order for close to $1,000. After they received that order, they called to ask me my rates to fly to Australia and train some of their staff in person. None of this would have happened if I didn't have the book available for sale on Amazon.

What should you do? Put everything you offer on Amazon.

Offering Free Chapters

If people you have really strong material, allow people to download and print up a few chapters of your e-book. This is a common practice of many savvy information marketers. Make two chapters available in downloadable form where people can go to the web, download the material, and can read those chapters. If you can deliver the goods in those two chapters, there is a good chance are they'll buy the whole book.

This method allows potential customers three options when they go to your site. They can either buy immediately, request to be put on your email list, OR to download a couple of free chapters to check you out.

This is a good idea that's worth testing if you have a book or ebook in your arsenal of info-products. AND if you've been following my advice, you certainly should.

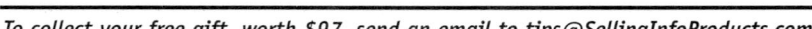

OTHER IMPORTANT ISSUES

Your Product Catalogue

You must put together a descriptive catalog that lists any or all of your products. You can see a sample of mine at the back of this book. Don't try and reinvent the wheel, if you've got a large selection of products, just copy the format that I've used in this book. If the number of products that you offer is limited then put a longer description of each product. I use a short description of each product only because of the volume of products that I'm promoting.

Someone called me the other day to buy a self storage book. I said, "You know, I don't really know if the book is the best thing for you. Can you tell me a little about your situation and why you want a book?" And he said "Well, I own a management company and we're starting to move over from real estate and going to be managing self-services." I said "Oh really? How many do you think you'll be managing?" "Oh, maybe three or four to begin with." I said, "Really? Well, I don't then think that the book is really the best thing for you. But I'll throw in the book for free if you buy something else. Why don't you take a look at some of the packages I'm going to e-mail over to you?"

So, I e-mailed him my catalog and within 20 minutes I had an order for $776.00. He wanted the book for $99.00. What do we call that? We call it an "upsell". Now, you don't want to upsell someone where it's not appropriate. You only want to upsell when you believe that your products are going to help them.

You need a catalog for all of your products per niche in both an online and offline form. Let me repeat that. You need a catalog of all your products per niche in both an online and offline form. This means that you need to have a physical catalog with pages and you also need to have an online catalog in PDF version, so that you can email to a prospect. Every once in a while you're going to get a customer who's not real computer savvy and won't be able to figure out how to read the PDF file. Therefore, in each email you send to someone that contains a PDF attachment, you need to explain that you need the adobe acrobat reader to read the file and send them to www.adobe.com to download the reader. Be sure to inform them that you can download the reader for free and that they do not need to be worried about viruses. If you include this with every email, you won't be deluged with people unable to open the file.

The product catalogue needs to list benefits in bullet form for each product that you are selling. That's the "FULL" product catalog. The one at the back of this book is the short form version of the catalog. With either one, give people the best highlights of the products that you have. What makes them so good? Why are they good? What are the 7 things you need to know? What are the 11 things to avoid? It's great to put in numerical lists. People like to have lists of positives and negatives. They'll look through your bullet points and will buy the entire product based on 1 bullet. They will look through the list and say "Eureka! That's it!"

To be even more impressive, put in a bullet point and tell people exactly where they can find that information in your document or what tape it's on. You can produce some really high-voltage excitement. Your customers will be able to say, "I want that and I know where it is! It's on the 3rd tape, and as soon as I get it, I'm going to listen to the 3rd tape."

Another feature of the catalog should be your offers for bundled products. Present your products a la carte, but them give people incentives for ordering a SET of your products that are related. This increases the average order size. This is one of the most important points you will learn in this book if you're selling information products.

When someone calls my office and they want to buy something from me, I have one goal. My goal is to increase the average size of the order in an ethical fashion. In other words, if they can't afford it or if it isn't appropriate, I won't upsell. I want to make sure that you understand that you need to provide them with offers that are so outstanding they'll be crazy if they don't buy it. For example, I might make an offer like get 3 for $197 or 6 for $297. That's an outrageous offer: it's much lower than what I typically sell them for. But by making this offer, I might increase my sales from one tape to 3 or 6.

I have two signs in my office, and I'd advise you to do the same. One sign says "Measurement eliminates argument." Somebody says to me "Well Fred, do you think this would work or this would work?" I say, "I don't know. Let's test it, let's find out. Let's look at the numbers."

The other sign says "Upsell Everything". If you have a product or a service that you're providing for people, make sure that when they say "Oh, well I'd like to order your self-storage book." that you have an upsell offer. Tell them, "That's nice. Because we have a special going through the end of this week. If you order the self-storage book today, you can get the videos, normally $195, for just $95. Can I add that to your order?"

It's like McDonalds: "Do you want fries with that?" What's happening here is we're doing it at a much higher level. That one action alone with a big company could literally increase their sales by 10%, maybe tens of millions of dollars. And a lot of companies don't do it. You'd better know, yourself, what the upsell is on every product. You'd better have your staff know, and you'd better tell anyone else answering the phone what they must do when a call comes in. Think about this for each product you offer: what's the upsell going to be? And if you have good stuff, you shouldn't be hesitant to sell.

Returns: Reducing them to VIRTUALLY Zero

I suggest that you offer people lifetime money-back guarantees. Whenever I tell that to clients, particularly bigger clients, they tend to freak out. They say "Oh my God. We can't offer a life-time money-back guarantee." Let me give you the data on this. It's been tested across industries and across markets. Offering lifetime guarantees will increase your sales by such a large factor that if there are any additional returns, they will be completely outweighed by the number of additional sales.

By offering a lifetime money-back guarantee your sales might go up 30%, and your returns go up 10%. The net is that you make a whole lot more money. In other words, yes, you might get some returns and you probably will get a few more returns by offering a really intense guarantee. But it is worth it in overall net sales.

Have you seen on TV how they offer 30-day money-back guarantees? That's crazy. You know what happens when people buy those products? They literally mark the calendar and say, "I've got 30 days. I've got to be really careful with this product because I want to be able to send it back." A lot of those products get returned. Increase that guarantee to a year and then to a lifetime. If your products are good, they will rarely ever come back.

I'm not suggesting that you should be selling things to people that they don't need or want and hoping that they forget about it. But I'll tell you what, not offering people a strong guarantee will hurt you and hurt your sales.

Often with software, once you open the package you cannot return it. You want to be different. If you've got a damned good product, you want to offer a guarantee so strong even Microsoft doesn't do it.

Everything I sell, like everything you sell, should have a lifetime guarantee. The one thing that makes me have more agita than anything else in the world is seeing products come back. It makes me sick to my stomach. It happens very infrequently; my return rates are really low. But it makes me really sick. And it makes me feel like I either sold something to somebody who shouldn't have bought it, or I didn't do the job right. Deliver easy-to-use, understandable products that are packed with great content. That is your key to reducing your return rates to zero.

There will always be a few people who take and copy your stuff and return it. That's life. If they do it twice, don't remove them from your database, but put a "Do Not Sell" order in their file on your database. In other words, you want to be able to stop them from buying and then returning. And I have to admit, I have occasionally done something that you will probably think was sort of cruel. I had to figure out some way to get back at someone. And I did it in sort of a subtle way. Here's what I did.

Someone who was on the "Do Not Sell" list because they had returned stuff and it was obvious that they were playing games. So I sent out an individual letter making it look like it was a mass mailing, just to this person, making them this outrageous offer. Like normally $5,000 today and today only, it's $2! And they called up to order it and I said "Oh God. You know, I'm really sorry because you had returned a couple of others, we're not honoring that offer for you." I wanted to teach him a lesson.

You never, I repeat, never want you to delete the person from your list because by deleting the person from your database, because then you don't remind yourself that you don't want their business. I had this happen just the other day with someone who had written a bad check and copied and returned products. He calls up real chipper "Hey Fred! How you doing?" Once I found out who it was, I said, "Oh, yeah. What ever happened to that bounced check? You still bouncing checks? Because it's really dangerous. If you don't make good on that stuff, people will never sell to you. In fact, did you know that those of us in the information marketing business have a "black list" that we put people on? We all trade that kind of information. So, I'd be really careful about that."

He says, "What are you talking about?" I said "What do you mean, what am I talking about?" I said "You bounced a check to us. You never made good on it." We literally called 8 or 10 times, sent him 4, 5 or 6 e-mails; got no response. Now, he's calling 8, 9 months later, acting like everything's okay. You know what he then did, when we wouldn't sell to him? He got a friend to order it and we wouldn't fulfill that order either. It got comical because I was actually quite impressed that he would go to such lengths to get hold of my material. Even to having a friend put it on his credit card and then pay the guy for it.

Preventing THEFT of Your Intellectual Property

People in the business of selling information are always concerned about people stealing their information. It's a valid concern, but remember what the law says: Ideas are NOT copyrightable. Only the specific presentation of those ideas. If you find a book on a given topic and want to write a book on the same topic, go right ahead. Just don't copy the specific words. That's plagiarism.

In this Internet age, let's understand reality. If someone likes your e-book and wants to share it with a friend, or two, or ten, there is very little you can do about it. However, you can set things up so you actually make more sales when people do this.

A certain number of people will take and "share" your information with others. Accept this as reality. Don't fight it. Encryption or password-protection won't eliminate this. So what do you do? Instead, imbed offers into your products. You want to mention 800 numbers, and give offers only to "registered users". Let me repeat that. You want to give offers to registered users. What does that mean? Somebody who has actually bought and paid for it and they would have a receipt to prove it.

What will that do? Somebody gets it and sees an offer, or a bonus. It says: "As a registered user, you get this and this and this. " The person who copied the product goes "Oh man. I really want that." What are they going to do? They have to call up and order their own version of the product to get it.

Expect people to be dishonest. That's human nature. Understanding that you can take advantage of this fact.

A Few Words of Wisdom About Online Sales

I want to give you two words of wisdom on online ordering here and they're really two very important things. The first is to never send people to a web site. Send them to an e-mail address. Let me explain to you why. If someone goes to a web site, there is a less than 100% chance you will capture their e-mail address because they have to sign up for something or agree to get something. If you send someone to an e-mail address, by definition you have captured 100% of their e-mail addresses.

One of the biggest mistakes being made out in the world right now in online marketing is people sending people to web sites. Because your percentage rate of e-mail address, by definition, has to be less than 100%. If you send someone to an e-mail address, by definition you've captured their e-mail address. Everybody understand that? It's a very, very profound point.

If I tell you to visit my web site www.SeminarExpert.com, is there a chance you may not sign up for my daily message? However, if I send you to tips@SeminarExpert.com, what happens? You have signed up for my tips.

But what if the person needs a little more information? I want them to get the information via my auto responder series. My auto responder series is giving them information. Do they have enough information that they don't have to look at your site? No. I first send them to the Tips site and then, if they go on to look at the web site, that's delightful. But I'm not going to direct them to my site. I'm going to direct them to an e-mail address so I can capture it.

How do you send somebody to an e-mail address? Send me an e-mail at tips@SeminarExpert.com. Send me an e-mail at tips@xyz.com. All you need to do is send me an e-mail. Let's say that I'm on the radio. Somebody says, "How do we get in touch with you?" I say well any of your listeners who want to get my free 7-day course on How to Market and Promote Their Own Seminars all you have to do is send an e-mail to tips@SeminarExpert.com, and I'll put you on that free 7-day course. The first seven messages they get are that free 7-day course I promised them.

Now, believe me folks, I didn't invent all this stuff myself so don't look at me like I'm the genius. I'm copying and combining a lot of other people's stuff here. But this works. If you're on a radio show, if you're in a position to get people to buy something, you send them to an e-mail address; you do not send them to a web site. That's the first thing.

The second item that I promise you is very crucial and important was told to me by somebody and this is really, really brilliant. Barnes and Noble is doing nine hundred million dollars offline at their bookstores. They're doing probably 100 million dollars online. That means the ratio of offline to online business is still 9 or 10 to 1. So if you have an online business, you sure as heck better have an offline business. Why? Because if you're not you're neglecting 90% of the market.

I have a client that's 19 years old that I'm coaching. He's on his second business. Sold his first business, before he turned 18, for a million dollars. He's got a site that he's working on for people who fish. He sells fishing lures. He's got a whole online presence set up and now he wants to set up a series of offline retail stores. Why? Because he said to me, "Fred, look at the numbers. Even a successful online company usually does 900% more business offline than they do online. Why would I ever want to neglect my offline business? Not only that, but the two tend to work together." This is a nineteen year old kid. Is it any wonder he's already a millionaire?

Sharper Image is another great example. You buy Sharper Image products online; you have a Sharper Image store. The two work together; hand in glove. It's a great philosophy. Don't ever forget if you have an online business, you must have an offline portion of it as well, if it makes sense. In most cases, it does. An example of it not making sense would be Travelocity. You wouldn't want or need to have Travelocity stores.

You don't have to open a retail store; you could just as easily get someone offline to promote your products or a store to sell them for you. This could be an example of an affiliation. Don't neglect offline business when you're doing online.

Branding

Everyone talks about branding. Do you know what? Branding for anyone who has less that $100 million to spend on advertising is stupid. But if you can brand while you are self-liquidating, that's fine. In other words, if you can break even on the sale of a product and get your name out there, that's delightful.

If you ever hear anyone talk to you about branding, just say "Brand this!" I mean, that's bogus because branding is really only a marketing concept that should be used by the large McDonalds of the world, the Goodyear's of the world, the Nike's of the world. Those people can think about branding. You and I have to think about a method of creating dollar for dollar expenditures; if we spend money on this, we make it back on that. None of this branding stuff. If we get branded in the process, great, but we got to think about direct sale methodologies.

Packaging

All of the products that you sell will have to be packaged in something. That's not ENTIRELY true. On occasion, I have put rubberbands around audio tapes and then sold them. In doing this I can legitimately reduce prices because of a LACK of packaging. I do this infrequently, but I do it. For the most part you're going to have your products packaged. No matter what you decide to do, try and standardize them. Let me explain why.

I have standardized my book sizes. That way, my books have a consistent look to them. The main reason, however, is shipping. The ability to ship in the same size container and have all the books stay together nicely and neatly prevents books from getting damaged and keeps the shipping costs down. They are also less apt to get damaged when they are shipped.

As far as audio-cassettes, you have some different options. I have opted to put my audio programs that have a workbook with them in a binder with a three-hole punch works best. Do not go beyond 35 pages for the printed matter because that drives up your cost dramatically. If you need to have other printed matter for people to examine, send them to a website to download a PDF document or attach a CD-rom with all of the extra printed matter.

I'm moving in the direction of NOT sending people a manual, but instead, including a CD with all of the printed matter that I'm including. This will reduce both the cost of printing and shipping. Let people print the manual out themselves. Sell it from the standpoint of being able to access the information on their computers. This will also allow you to imbed offers that have your affiliate links where you can make money from referring them to a certain vendor.

For the cassettes I use very simple and basic cassette holders that are provided to me by Blackbourne. They are plastic trays with a 3-hole punch on one side of the trays. I put these in the binders (I use 1 inch binders I get from Office Max) along with the printed matter. I then shrinkwrap the binders.

I also use 60 minute cassettes for every program. Why? Because if I'm ordering more masters or more copy tapes, I only have to order one thing and I don't get confused. This way, you can't reach into the closet and make a mistake!! The cassette masters and copy tapes are bought from Kingdom. There contact info is listed in the Million Dollar Rolodex at the back of the book.

For CD's they have a variety of different packaging available. Whatever you decide on, just stick to the same packaging.

Since every product I produce has an ISBN number associated with them I sticker the products on both the package itself and outside in the same place on the outside of the shrink-wrap. This way, if the shrink wrap comes off, it will still have the ISBN number sticker on the product itself. This is particularly important when you sell products through Amazon. This is how they expect them.

I get the stickers for the ISBN numbers at a place called Fotel (www.Fotel.com). They can produce labels for you with minimum quantities of 100 pieces. They can also turn them around in less than a week.

As far as videos go, you can do one of three things. You can either have video sleeves customized and printed. If you're going to sell 1,000 or more units, this is worth considering. If not, you can either use cardboard plain video sleeves or plastic Video sleeves.

With DVDs there are standard plastic boxes which you can use. These cases are set up to allow you to put in anywhere from 1 – 24 units.

Rich Rubinstein at www.TapeDuplicatorMan.com can help you to both design and duplicate your audio cassettes, CD's and DVD's. I've consulted with him on this process and he understands how to do things for both me and myclients (that includes YOU now).

Fulfillment

After you create your products and start selling them, the next step is to get them into your buyers hands as quickly and inexpensively as possible. Many of your products will be digital, but in order to do things right you're going to want to do create a combination of physical and digital products. A hybrid product like I talked about earlier. You immediately deliver to people your digital product and then you follow up with a physical component to your product.

When you first start out, you're probably going to be doing all of your fulfillment yourself. Fulfillment means physically delivering the products to the customers. As you do more and more business you'll be able to hire someone to handle this aspect of your business.

I still use the US Post Office for mailing all of my materials. I use priority mail with delivery receipt confirmation. Whether you choose to use them or another carrier, make sure you use some system that has a means to confirm delivery of your products and materials.

When you first get started you won't be able to afford to use an outside company to handle your fulfillment. Over time you should be concentrating your efforts on creating and marketing your info products. It is time much better spent.

Companies that offer this fulfillment service send the products out for you. They generally don't handle small quantities. If you do find a company that will do a small quantity, they'll usually charge you a ridiculous rate.

Again, I HIGHLY recommend that you contact my friend and client Rich Rubinstein at www.TapeDuplicatorMan.com. He will not only do your duplicating, he'll also do fulfillment. Rich is a Psychiatrist who decided to get into the information business. He is the consummate professional and comes with my highest recommendation. His company does both fulfillment and duplication.

When you get to the point where you want someone else to being doing your fulfillment, Rich is the guy to talk to.

Here's the problem I had that might be yours as well. You may find that doing your own fulfillment very time consuming, BUT, you can't afford to have someone else do it because it's too expensive. You will have to set up your own system for handling this until you get successful enough to pay a fulfillment company. If you have your systems set up effectively it will take you less time and be much more efficient.

Do I have a specific system that I suggest you use? No. This is so individual that suggesting that you copy mine won't be very helpful.

An order can come in via a live seminar, phone, fax or online. The key to your system is consistency. Doing it the same way each time. Once you figure out your system then codify it. Put it down on paper. Create a flow chart to remind yourself, or show others, exactly what has to happen each time an order comes in.

The key to NON online orders is the order sheet itself. For orders that come in via a live seminar, phone or fax, a "standard" physical order form should be used.

When an order comes in via phone, I grab an order sheet for that industry and fill it out as if I were sitting next to the customer face to face. I then enter their credit card number and expiration date along with all of their pertinent information on the order sheet well.

I then go to my computer database (Filemaker Pro) and input the customer information into my database segmented by industry. I will then be able to print my packing labels from here as well.

Orders that come in via a live event or by fax will be filled out by the customers themselves. This is both good and bad. Good in that you have less work in most cases, bad when you can't read peoples' handwriting.

After I've gotten the order sheet, I then pull the products off the shelf and put it into a priority mail box of the appropriate size. Make sure that you have a sufficient supply of products on the shelf so you don't have to go off and duplicate a product just to fulfill it for a single order.

Once your package is ready to go to the post office I add a delivery confirmation receipt and put the name of the person who ordered, the product or products ordered and their zip code. After taking the boxes to the Post Office I bring back the delivery confirmation receipts and staple them to a duplicated copy of the order sheet that I've made.

I then file these order sheets alphabetically in a "shipped order" file. I keep the orders for the year in an active file. At the end of the year,

I transfer all of this hard copy to an archived file in my garage. Chances are I won't have to look for an order unless someone has a problem. If this does happen, I only have to look in this year's order file or in the garage.

That's my process. You'll develop your own. BUT, remember, the best use of your time is to develop and market your information products, not doing fulfillment. As soon as you possibly can, have someone else (who is reliable) do it.

Shrink-Wrap

If you're selling anything on Amazon other than books you'll need to shrink wrap the items before you send them. So, you'll need to buy a shrink wrap machine. Take a look at: http://www.ajminc.com to get some good prices on some of the standard equipment you'll need.

It will consist of basically three things: the bag, the sealer and the heater. They will provide you with plastic-type see through bags of different sizes that you "drop" the product into. They will also give you a machine that will seal the bag closed and cut off the excess. You'll also get a device that looks like a blow-dryer.

Make sure you buy bags big enough to fit your products into easily. Remember to consider the depth, width AND height of what you're selling. Assuming you have the right size you drop the product into the bag (with the ISBN number directly on the product), then seal the bag with the sealer and use the blow-dryer to "shrink" the bag down to fit snugly on the product.

Make sure that you then attach your ISBN number sticker on both the outside of the shrink wrap AND on the inside (on the product itself). Shrink wrapping will protect your product and assure the ISBN sticker stays attached.

Selling Your Products Through Others: Licensing Options

Before the days of the internet (remember those days?), many people still sold other people's products. The old term used to be a dealer. The internet updated term is an affiliate. Having an affiliate means that other people are selling your products for you on a straight commission basis. If someone sells something, great, if they don't, who cares? People only get paid if they sell something.

There are a number of ways to get affiliates to come to you. One of the best ways to do this is to go to the search engines with your keywords and find other people that are selling similar or related products.

For example, for radiopublicity.com, one of the things I told Alex to do and one of the things I helped do for him as a coach, was to look up "radio publicity". We looked up the top 100 names that came up in the search engines. Then I sent an email to each one of these names. I e-mailed them and said "Hey. I don't know if you know this but my buddy, Alex Carroll, has got this great site called radiopublicity.com and you can be an affiliate and you can make up to $500 every time you make a sale." By the way, all of you reading this book should become affiliates for the program. If somebody buys a $1,000 package through you, you get five hundred dollars. It's a great program if you want to do your own radio publicity.

You can set yourself up as an affiliate at places that you know of and believe in. But also, get other people to set themselves up as affiliates with you. Go to the search engines, put in the keywords and then contact those people. Do not send some kind of mass email – you should customize it. In other words, if I found you as number 56 on the list at Google under "radio publicity", I would say something like "Hey. I was looking on the web and I discovered your site, and I particularly liked this part of the site and I really think that radio publicity, if you take a look at it might be a good match because of x, y or z."

If you send out something that looks like a generic e-mail, you're going to get a much lower rate of response. Whereas, if you make it a little customized, you will get much better results. Look at the site first, make sure there's a match and then proceed.

Do people have to be in a relevant business or in a related field in order to have them set up as affiliates? The answer is, no, not if you have no investment of time and money. I'll set up everybody and their brother as an affiliate as long as it doesn't cost me anything. However, if I were to go into a Wal-Mart store and have to pay $3,000 a month and pay an employee, then I would have to make a decision as to whether or not Wal-Mart is the proper outlet for whatever it is I'm selling.

Let's say for example you trust me, you've bought tons of stuff from me and I send you an e-mail that says "You know what? I just found this incredible bicycle wrench. Man, this is the best bicycle wrench ever made. If you own a bicycle, you need to have this wrench. Click here." You'd probably go "OK. Fred, you know, I trust him. He's given me good stuff in the past", and then click. It makes sense. An affiliate program can be like that. Do business with people you trust.

In addition to having people become affiliates for your product, there is another method called licensing. Licensing is when people give you an up-front bunch of cash for a license to sell your product outright. In order to understand how a license works, let's take my program How to Market and Sell Information Products to Make You Filthy Rich. If any one of you wanted to take this program and become a licensee I would sell you what is called a "standard license". A standard license usually goes for between ten and fifteen times the standard retail price. So, if I were going to sell this program for $197.00, then the standard license would be sold for between $2000 and $2500.

As the licensee, what do you get for that money? The standard license usually includes the product, the sales letter that sells the product and a couple of bonuses. You get the license to make as many copies as you want and you are allowed to sell them for whatever amount you want.

Why would you choose to become a licensee? Let's go back to this program as an example. Let's say you've already given me $2,000 for the license. Every time you duplicate the program it will cost you around $8 for the supplies. If you sell the program for $197, like I would, you will make $189 for each sale. By the time you sell your eleventh copy of the program, you have paid back your initial investment and are earning pure profit. So, in some cases, it makes a lot of sense to license products. This is true especially if you don't have any products of your own to sell when you begin.

I used to think "Well, if I license a product to Mr. Jones, he can make as many copies as he wants and sell them to people. I don't want to do that because they could be buying from me and I will be losing money." I was really off base with these thoughts. The chances of selling to the same people that will buy from Mr. Jones are quite slim. Secondly, if Mr. Jones sells 100,000 units of my product, what's it going to do to my business? It is going to increase it! Remember, I have bounce back offers in all of my products. I have the opportunity to add a percentage of those people that Mr. Jones captures to my OWN funnel! If Mr. Jones sells $100,000 worth of my product, God bless him! I don't care if he only paid $2000 for the license and ends up making a million dollars off my product. He is getting my name out there and helping me fill my funnel!

Now, there is one more kind of license called a master license. If I sell Mr. Jones a master license, he has the right to turn around and sell licenses to Mr. Smith. The cost of a master license is between 30 and 50 times the standard retail price of your product. You want to make sure, however, to sell a limited number of master licenses – the usual limit is between 10 and 20. How is Mr. Jones going to make his money? He can make it just as above AND he can make money selling standard licenses to other individuals. If he paid me $9000 for the master license and then found 5 people to buy a standard license from him, he will have earned his initial investment back. Since he can sell as many standard licenses as he wishes, the rest is profit – pure gravy!

Do you see the differences between the licenses? The standard license is selling the rights to remarket and sell that product. Selling a master license is the right to sell other licenses.

Some people, like McDonalds, sell you a master license with a yearly renewal fee (only they call it a franchise fee). I sell my licenses for life. Now why would I do that? I have two main reasons. The first is for the cash flow. If you give me a check for $9000, I don't have to work as hard this month. The second reason is that if you pay me $9000 I can be pretty sure that you're are going to sell a bunch of standard licenses and my name is going to get out there. I am more interested in getting my funnel filled!

I personally choose to sell a lot of licensed products. Let me explain why. Let's say I'm in the video producing industry and I'm selling them a variety of different products. Then I learn that "Ed" has a great product for video producers. Rather than create a similar product, which takes time and money and perhaps some knowledge or skill that I do not have, or go in a joint venture situation where I make 50% of product sales, I will elect to buy a standard license. In this way, I can sell as many copies of the product as I like and within a short amount of time, I will have paid back the licensing fee and be in the black, making a lot more money!! Selling licensed products gives me a lot more products to sell. I can use them as bonuses or freebies. It is a great deal for me. And it is a great deal for people like "Ed" because their name is going out among clientele in their niche!

Buyers Tend to Buy the Same Way

People who start out buying online, will tend to buy online again. The same is true of every other way that people can buy from you. They've done a lot of marketing studies in this area, but I always do my own marketing research at every seminar I do. I ask people to raiser their hands if they have ever bought a product via a television infomercial. The hands go up. I then ask people to keep them up if they have bought more than once that way. Inevitably, over 90% of the hands stay up.

Why? People find a method of buying that they are comfortable with and they tend to continue buying that same way. We are all creatures of habit and have certain buying behaviors that we have either learned or favor.

How is this information valuable to you if you sell information products? Simple. If someone buys a product from you through direct mail, make sure and continue to send them offers through the mail.

It doesn't mean that this person will NEVER buy using a different buying channel, but it tells us that we should continue to market to them in that manner since they have demonstrated that they DO buy that way. Don't totally neglect the other possible ways they might buy, but concentrate on the ways that they have demonstrated they will buy.

SELLING MORE
AND MORE OFTEN

Most businesses spend the vast majority of their time tying to find new customers. New customers are a necessary, but acquiring them is expensive. There is a far more effective means of increasing your revenue as an information marketer than being on a constant search for new customers.

Selling More

Each time someone is about to buy something from you, you MUST present them with the opportunity to buy MORE from you. This is the "do you want fries with that" portion of the ordering process. Not everyone will go for your upsell, but if ANY of them do, you've made more money from them than you would have made without this offer.

This is one of the single most neglected areas on the part of information marketers as a group. Why? Frankly, it's because of laziness. I have to admit that everything I sell does NOT have an upsell associated with it. This is dumb. But frankly, it's because I'm making enough money that I don't care as much. Bad idea.

So don't do as I do, do as I say. Make sure that every product you sell has an upsell to it. Don't have another product of your own to upsell people to? No problem. Offer them someone else's product that you remarket. You won't make as much money, but at least you'll make some of what you deserve.

The moral of this story? Keep producing lots of product to sell and to upsell.

To collect your free gift, worth $97, send an email to tips@SellingInfoProducts.com

Selling More Often

Once you have a group of customers, never underestimate their interest in spending more money with you. Some of the most successful marketers (including myself), have customers that have their credit cards on file with us. When we release a new product, the first thing we do is go to each of their credit cards and charge them for the newest and latest product we've created. It's almost stealing.

The biggest reason why people don't send their customers a lot of offers is they are scared to offend them. Rubbish! If you send people great offers for great products you can hit them up on a monthly or even weekly basis. Those who don't want to buy will look, but not pony up their money. Rarely, if ever, will these folks be offended.

The only time you will offend people with multiple offers is when you try and sell them CRAP. If you sell them great stuff, you'll virtually never get people annoyed at you.

With the two items I've just given you, you should be able to immediately increase your sales by 20-50%. That's right. Simply by offering upsells and presenting your customers with good offers more often you can generate a whole lot more money for yourself. Now, go out and to it!

To upsell the MOST effectively you need to get as many people as you can to add the LARGEST amount of dollars

CONCLUSION

Here's what I want to leave you with.

- Selling info products is a great business and it will continue to get better. Why will it continue to get better? It's going to get more profitable. As we continue to find better and faster ways to deliver digital audio and digital video over the net, our costs will go down, our profits will go up and it will be a tremendous boon for info marketers.

- Create your systems before you start, not after. It's much easier to set up your systems before you start rather than afterwards, because if you do, you'll have the whole thing nailed and you won't be playing catch up. You can just plug in new products and finding your next niche. Get started with webmarketingmagic now.

- You have to set up a system that's web-based. It's cheaper and less hassle. It's less aggravation. It's automatic. You don't have to do it manually. It makes a lot of sense.

- Get started now, even if you sell other people's products. All of you now have the ability to take my products and resell them as a dealer at 50% off. You can license the products. I'll even give you a special deal as a book buyer. Generate your own leads, sell them my products and collect the commission. I did the same thing with other people's products when I started. Get selling! Sell something!

- You need to develop your own products as soon as possible. Even if you start marketing my products or someone else's products, you need to develop and sell your own products as quickly as possible. You'll make more money. What was the first items that I sold? I sold a little book and a set of tapes called "Investing for

Beginners: A Practical Approach in Plain English". You can tell it was a long time ago because in the picture on the back of the book, I had a full head of hair! That was back in 1984.

- Once you've done all of the other elements above your primary role is to drive traffic to your site using both online and offline techniques that suit your personality and style.

- Make a whole lot of money and have a whole lot of fun. If you don't, it's not worth it.

Thanks for taking the time to read this book. I've given you everything that I know. I haven't held back anything hoping that you would buy something else from me. I want you to succeed. I want you to have fun. Go out there and get started today!

Other Valuable Learning Resources from Fred Gleeck

How to Self Publish Your Own Book, Get Famous and Make Well Over $250K a Year

This one-day seminar on audio-tape will give you a complete overview of the self-publishing process. It will provide you with everything you need to get your book written and printed AND start developing and marketing a back end line of other products and services.

For More info go to: www.SelfPublishingSuccess.com

Marketing and Promoting Your Own Seminar and Workshops

Whether you're a speaker, author or consultant, seminars can be a very attractive source of additional revenue. There's only one problem. You can lose a lot of money if you don't what you're doing. This program will show you exactly how to promote your own events and make money doing it. I've done over 1300 one-day events myself!

For More info go to: www.SeminarExpert.com

How to Make $5,000 a Day as a Professional Speaker

If you want to really make a living from professional speaking, you NEED this program. In a fast moving interview, Fred Gleeck reveals the secrets of how to get started and thrive as a speaking professional. Other programs may give you part of the story, this program gives you the whole story!

For More info go to: www.ProfessionalSpeakingSuccess.com

Creating and Selling Information Products

If you're an information marketer, you need to create information products to be truly successful. Not only will creating products enhance your image; it will also allow you to make money while you sleep. This program will show you how to turn your products into a solid money making machine that requires a minimum of effort.

For More info go to: www.SellingInfoProducts.com

How to Start and Build a Turbo-Charged Consulting Business

If you have expertise in a topic, you can get paid for that expertise as a consultant. Most consultants spend their time chasing down prospects that have no interest in

---

To collect your free gift, worth $97, send an email to tips@SellingInfoProducts.com

their services. This one-day seminar on audio-tape will show you the right way to prospect for high dollar customers and get paid while you're doing it.

For More info go to: www.ConsultingExpert.com

24 Direct Marketing Secrets to Your Professional Services Business

If you market any service whatsoever, this is a program you can use. You'll get the inside secrets on how to do marketing that REALLY works. It's called direct marketing. It's the only kind of marketing I do. It's the only kind of marketing you'll want to do after you listen to this program. It's packed with highly relevant useable ideas.

For More info go to: www.DirectMarketingExpert.com

How to Double Your Sales on the Web in 90 Days or Less

If you want to make your website successful you have to do two things. First, you have to design a site that REALLY sells. Secondly, you have to find an effective way to drive traffic to your site. The problem is that most people don't truly know how to do either effectively. This program will show you how to do both!

For More info go to: www.WebMarketingSolution.com

How to Get Your Own Radio Show in 7 Days or Less

If you'd like to host your own radio show, you can! In this audio program I interview Mike Litman on how to get your own radio show in under a week. YOU can be on the radio in a fraction of the time you thought possible following these step by step instructions.

For More info go to: www.GetYourOwnRadioShow.com

How to Make ANY Product an Amazon Best Seller

If you'd like to turn your book, audio or video into an Amazon best seller, this is the program for you. You'll learn the inside secrets to catapult your product onto the top of the Amazon charts.

For More info go to: www.CreateYourBestSeller.com

How to Start Your Own Association

Starting your own association will give you tons of benefits. Among them, you can appoint yourself the president and get instant credibility in your field. This program will show you how to do virtually everything to do just that.

For More info go to: www.StartYourOwnAssociation.com

How to Run Your Own Conferences

Want to create and market your own conferences? This is the program that will show you how. I interview a top expert in the field and get him to "spill the beans" on exactly how to run highly profitable conferences and large events.

For More info go to: www.RunYourOwnConferences.com

Writing Effective Web Copy

Want to get your web copy to close a higher percentage of visitors to do what you want? It's tough, but you'll learn how to do exactly that in this fast moving interview of internet marketing maven, Terry Dean.

For More info go to: www.WebCopyMagic.com

Creating Highly Profitable Joint Ventures

Joint ventures are how many people have made their fortunes. You too can learn the secrets to making them work for you as well. This fast paced interview with Terry Dean will give you the formula for success with JV's.

For More info go to: www.JointVentureGenius.com

Info Products Bootcamp

This 22 hour audio program will give you everything you need to start and build a successful information products business. If you have specific knowledge in your field, why not package and get paid for it?

For More info go to: www.InfoProductsSeminar.com

Seminar on Seminars Bootcamp

Want to market and promote your own seminar? This 3 day information packed event on audio will show you exactly how to do it yourself. Soup to nuts, this program will walk you through the seminar business from A to Z.

For More info go to: www.SeminarOnSeminars.com

Making Big Money Using Google

Learn how to use Google and specifically Google Ad words to drive loads of traffic to your site. This fascinating interview with Perry Marshall will give you everything you need to succeed.

For More info go to: www.TheGoogleExpert.com

For the latest products that I offer, please go to www.FredGleeck.com. This site will give you the latest listings of all of my products and services. Make sure to get on my ezine list to receive special offers by sending an email to tips@SellingInfoProducts.com

ORDER SHEET

Product	Price	Qty.	Subtotal
How to Self Publish Your Own Book and Get Famous	$97	_____	_____
Marketing and Promoting Your Own Seminar and Workshops	$97	_____	_____
How to Make $5,000 a Day as a Professional Speaker	$97	_____	_____
Creating and Selling Information Products	$97	_____	_____
How to Start and Build a Turbo-Charged Consulting Business	$97	_____	_____
24 Direct Marketing Secrets to Your Professional Services Business	$97	_____	_____
How to Double Your Sales on the Web in 90 Days or Less	$97	_____	_____
How to Get Your Own Radio Show in 7 Days or Less	$97	_____	_____
How to Make ANY Product a Best Seller	$97	_____	_____
How to Start Your Own Association	$97	_____	_____
How to Run Your Own Conferences	$97	_____	_____
Writing Effective Web Copy	$97	_____	_____
Creating Highly Profitable Joint Ventures	$97	_____	_____

Please CIRCLE your choices!

Package A: Any 3 items from the list above (and 1 hour of consulting time) $297

Package B: Any 5 items from the list above (and 2 hours of consulting time) $497

Package C: The "whole enchilada" $777

Everything on this list PLUS: 3 hours of one on one consulting (face to face or on the phone); unlimited email assistance; and 50% off any additional products or services

Info Products Bootcamp Audios (close to 24 hours of material) $497

Seminar on Seminars Audios (a full three days of content) $497

TOTAL: Please add $3 per item (per program – not per package) for Shipping ..... $ _____

Guarantee: EVERYTHING we sell comes with a no B.S, money back, lifetime guarantee. If you're not happy, SEND IT BACK!

(Please Print)

Name: _____

Company: _____

Address: _____

City: _____ State: _____ Zip: _____

Phone:_____ E-mail:_____

_____ VISA _____ MC _____ Amex _____ Enclosed is my check (payable to Fred Gleeck)

Account No.: _____ Expiration Date: _____

Signature: _____

(Charges will appear as Fred Gleeck Productions)

Please send this form along with your check or credit card information to:
Fred Gleeck Productions • 209 Horizon Peak Drive • Henderson, NV 89012
Phone: 800-345-3325 • Fax: 702-617-4278

ORDER SHEET

Product	Price	Qty.	Subtotal
How to Self Publish Your Own Book and Get Famous	$97	____	_____
Marketing and Promoting Your Own Seminar and Workshops	$97	____	_____
How to Make $5,000 a Day as a Professional Speaker	$97	____	_____
Creating and Selling Information Products	$97	____	_____
How to Start and Build a Turbo-Charged Consulting Business	$97	____	_____
24 Direct Marketing Secrets to Your Professional Services Business	$97	____	_____
How to Double Your Sales on the Web in 90 Days or Less	$97	____	_____
How to Get Your Own Radio Show in 7 Days or Less	$97	____	_____
How to Make ANY Product a Best Seller	$97	____	_____
How to Start Your Own Association	$97	____	_____
How to Run Your Own Conferences	$97	____	_____
Writing Effective Web Copy	$97	____	_____
Creating Highly Profitable Joint Ventures	$97	____	_____

Please **CIRCLE** your choices!

Package A: Any 3 items from the list above (and 1 hour of consulting time) $297

Package B: Any 5 items from the list above (and 2 hours of consulting time) $497

Package C: The "whole enchilada" $777

Everything on this list PLUS: 3 hours of one on one consulting (face to face or on the phone); unlimited email assistance; and 50% off any additional products or services

Info Products Bootcamp Audios (close to 24 hours of material) $497

Seminar on Seminars Audios (a full three days of content) $497

TOTAL: Please add $3 per item (per program – not per package) for Shipping . . . . . $ _____

Guarantee: EVERYTHING we sell comes with a no B.S, money back, lifetime guarantee. If you're not happy, SEND IT BACK!

(Please Print)

Name: _____

Company: _____

Address: _____

City: _____ State: _____ Zip: _____

Phone: _____ E-mail: _____

____ VISA ____ MC ____ Amex ____ Enclosed is my check (payable to Fred Gleeck)

Account No.: _____ Expiration Date: _____

Signature: _____

(Charges will appear as Fred Gleeck Productions)

Please send this form along with your check or credit card information to:
Fred Gleeck Productions • 209 Horizon Peak Drive • Henderson, NV 89012
Phone: 800-345-3325 • Fax: 702-617-4278

Your Complete Solution to Doing Business on the Web!
www.webmarketingmagic.com

Reasonably priced for all you get and you can pay either monthly or yearly! Try it out for a month for less than $5!

Here's What you get with this amazing program:

- **E-Book Module:** Deliver your digital products including e-books with virtually NO effort.

- **Shopping Cart:** As incredibly easy to use shopping cart even a Mac user like me can figure out!

- **Client Database System:** Keep all your customer records in one place sortable by a variety of fields.

- **Broadcast Module:** Allow you to send out a message to any segment of your database quickly and easily

- **Smart Auto-Responders:** Send people a virtually unlimited number of pre-programmed messages.

- **Forms Module:** Create a form for a variety of purposes (including surveys) quickly and easily.

- **Ad Tracker Module:** Track all your advertising by clicks and orders as well as "type-in traffic" to your site.

- **Coupon Module:** Set up and accurately track others who want to sell your products.

- **Affiliate Module:** Create urgency for your offers using either a time element or a specific number of units.

- **Tell a Friend Module**: Get others to refer people to your site with a few clicks for the mouse.

How do you get started?
Go to www.webmarketingmagic.com and sign up online!

Special Offer: Sign up for a full year of webmarketingmagic and get $97 worth of credit towards to purchase of any products of mine being sold for $200 or more.

No matter what you sell, this integrated program will help you to sell more of it! Take a look at some of the incredible features it contains. Also, you can do a 30 day trial for just $3.95. Give it a try!

To collect your free gift, worth $97, send an email to tips@SellingInfoProducts.com

How to Get in Touch with Me

If you need to contact me, the best way to do so is to email me. The best email address for me is fgleeck@aol.com. You can also reach me by calling 702-617-4205. If I'm not at that number my machine will tell you the best number to call to find me.

If you want to mail me something (like a gift for example), feel free to send it to my office in the Las Vegas area at:

Fred Gleeck
209 Horizon Peak Drive
Henderson, NV 89012

Also, if you produce any information products as a result of following my advice, please send me a copy. Preferably, one that's autographed by you.

Warning!!

On occasion I will get a call from a customer or prospect asking me about a particular product in the information marketing field. I know most of the players in the field and I'm always happy to give you my opinion.

As my "friend" Bill O'Reilly would say, here's the NO SPIN truth: 90% or more of all of the people selling marketing related products are crooks. What do I mean by this? I define a crook as someone who either intentionally defrauds people or someone who delivers much less value than what they promised.

There are some information marketers out there who shade the truth when they promote themselves, their products and their services. There are also others who are downright crooks.

Maybe you can make more money if you are willing to be a sleazy operator - if you're willing to play fast and loose with the facts. BUT, that's not for me. I keep my overhead very low and lead a pretty simple life. The net result? I don't have a huge "nut" to cover every month and don't have to make a sale to put a meal on the table.

I suspect that I'm different than other marketers in this area. When I go out to dinner with a lot of my peers, they want to eat at fancy restaurants and spend lots of cash. That's just not who I am. That doesn't make me any better, it just means that I don't have to pay those massive AMEX bills every month that all of my peers have to do to support a lifestyle like that.

Everyone has to be themselves. You are no exception. But I'll give you my secret for financial success in this business. Keep your overhead low and produce quality products. Then you can do what I do.

So, be careful when you deal with marketers in this field. There are a lot of people who aren't quite on the "up and up."

Want to Accelerate The Speed of Your Success?

I have two coaching programs that I've set up for people who want to learn how to "do" this business. One is a program that is geared to those people who want to "do it themselves." The other is geared to those who want to have me "hold their hands on a long term basis."

The do-it-yourself system involves a series of products on topics that are specifically relevant to helping you start and build a successful information product marketing business. Each package is customized to YOU.

Take a look at www.TheProductGuru.com for more information on both of these packages and see which one (if any) is right for you.

I also coach a select number of people each year on how to produce and market their own information products. It is a very expensive program and only for those who are truly serious about this business and willing to spend a lot of time and money to be successful.

It is not a program that you can just pay to get accepted. Not only do you have to have a niche or product line that I believe in, we also have to have a good personality match between us.

To give you the basic structure of the deal, you give me a fee up front and then pay me additional monies from the revenue that I help you start to generate. After you double what you have paid me, I then get a percentage of sales. If you have an interest, the best way to find out more about the program is to go to

But I warn you, the program is expensive and only geared to the truly serious.

If you're interested in either of these programs, call me at 702-617-4206 or go to www.TheProductGuru.com

Fred Gleeck's Million Dollar Rolodex
(Essential Contacts You'll Need – Tell them I sent you!)
Contacts you MUST use:

Domain Registration Services: www.UltraCheapDomains.com (LOW prices to register names)

Web Design: Phil Huff – www.PhilHuff.com

Web Hosting: www.Olm.net or Phil Huff (phil@philhuff.com)

Legal Matters: Stephe Soden – Soden and Steinberger 609-239-3200

Publicity: Alex Carroll (alex@RadioPublicity.com) and Paul Hartunian (Paul@Hartunian.com)

Copywriter: Jenny Hamby – jenny@hambycommunications.com; Sheri Waldrop – info@pro-scribe-writing.com

Book Cover Designer: Tami Dever – tamara@tlcgraphics.com

Book Cover Designer: Nick Zelinger – znick4@qwest.net - 303-985-4174

Editing/Ghostwriting: Call or email me for my latest and greatest recommendation

Small Business Accounting: Chris Trinka – 212-628-3139

Office Products: Viking Office Products – 800-421-1222

Computer Hardware: Mac/Micro Warehouse – 800-622-6222

Computer Software: NUBS (you MUST say you're a Fred Gleeck student) 800-231-6987

Duplicating Machines/Blank Media: Kingdom – www.Kingdom.com - 800-788-1122

Duplication/Fulfillment: Rich Rubinstein – www.DoctorDuplicator.com

Media Packaging: Sylvia Tapelt - Blackbourne – 888-676-6773

Contact Management Software: Act from Symantec or Filemaker Pro

Time Management Seminar: Franklin Covey – 800-487-1847

Audio Expert: Call or email me for my latest and greatest recommendation

Credit Card Merchant Accounts: check www.Google.com and put in the key words: "cheap merchant account"

Data Entry: Deborah (debdata@bellsouth.net) - 888-420-3282

To collect your free gift, worth $97, send an email to tips@SellingInfoProducts.com

Book You MUST Read:

Influence – Robert Cialdini
Jump Start Your Business Brain – Doug Hall
The Tipping Point – Malcolm Gladwell

Website References You MUST have:

www.WebMarketingMagic.com
automated system for doing business online

www.SeminarExpert.com
information on how to become a successful seminar promoter

www.SeminarOnSeminars.com
information on the bi-yearly seminar bootcamp

www.InfoProductsSeminar.com
information on the bi-yearly info products bootcamp

www.SelfPublishingSuccess.com
site showing how to maximize revenue as a publisher/author

www.ConsultingExpert.com
site that shows you how to make money as a consultant

www.TheProductGuru.com
site to find out about coaching in the information publishing arena

To get yourself on my email list:
Send a blank email to tips@SeminarExpert.com

ABOUT THE AUTHOR

Fred Gleeck has been speaking professionally for more than 15 years. He has a unique background that has contributed to his success.

Born in Japan and raised in the Philippines as the son of an American diplomat, he graduated from the University of Florida with high honors and a degree in marketing. His masters degree in international management is from the American Graduate school of International Management.

Fred moved to New York City after graduation where he was promptly fired from five major Fortune 500 companies in a row. There seemed to be unanimous agreement that he should be self-employed.

His first paid speaking engagement was one of his own public seminars that he promoted via a local newspaper ad.

Since then, Fred has given an average of 100 paid presentations a year for the past 15 years.

In addition to promoting his own seminars and workshops, he has also spoken for many of the major Fortune 500 companies. They include AT&T, IBM, Hewlett Packard, and Dow Chemical, to name a few.

Fred was CareerTrack's Top Trainer for four years in a row. He has authored three books and is working on three more.

Sign up for the free tips on professional speaking by sending an email to tips@professionalspeakingsuccess.com